Slaves wives and brides

Women under the rule of ISIS

JUDIT NEURINK

Copyright © 2018 Judit Neurink

All rights reserved.

Slaves wives and brides

Women under the rule of ISIS

Original title: The women of the Caliphate

Slaves, mothers and jihadi brides

Edited and updated in 2018

By Judit Neurink

English translation by Pamela Williams

Original Dutch version published by Uitgeverij Jurgen Maas in Amsterdam

First print October 2015

English version published by Amazon

First print September 2016

Copyright © Judit Neurink

Cover photo Eddy van Wessel,

Beds with Yazidi clothing in prison in Talafar

Photo author Adam Mirani

ISBN: 9781718116092

For Luisa, of whom we don't know who she is but we do know what she has had to endure; for Kayla, who did not survive and for Suaad, who has shared their mutual fate as a slave in the caliphate.

Other books by Judit Neurink in English

The Jewish Bride (novel, 2014)
The War of ISIS (non-fiction, 2015)
Women survive ISIS (long-read, 2015)
Violence recycled (non-fiction, 2021)
The Good Terrorist (novel. 2022)
A Devil's Child (novel, 2023)

CONTENTS

	Foreword	1
1	The Women of ISIS	5
2	Stolen, sold and raped	27
3	The woman and the ideology of ISIS	57
4	Woman against woman	91
5	Baghdadi's bride	109
6	Mothers of the caliphate	129
7	Recruiting in the West	153
8	Life under occupation	187
9	After ISIS	219
	Epilogue	255
	Word of Thanks	265
	List of sources	269

FOREWORD

For some time now ISIS has dominated the world news. We hear about acts of war and deaths as a result of bombings by a coalition in which western countries also participate, but also about human rights violations and the fate of thousands of stolen Yazidi women ISIS has imprisoned as sex slaves.

Women are the main victim in the cruel regime which the Iraqi ISIS leader Abu Bakr al-Baghdadi and his 'brothers' in 2014 managed to establish in parts of Syria and Iraq. Foremost – but not solely – the Yazidi women, whose situation we only know about through the stories of those who managed to successfully escape from the nightmare.

But what about the women who were living in the cities and villages controlled by ISIS, until the liberation of most of them in 2016 and 2017? And the women who could not prevent their men from joining the terrorist group, or whose sons allowed themselves to be recruited?

Next there were the women who are active on various levels in the caliphate, and those who did not voice protest against the rapes and abuses against the Yazidi women by the hands of their husbands and sons. Are they perpetrators or perhaps also victims? And what about the women from the West who were lured in by the false promise of being able to have a meaningful role for the new state?

This book puts all of these women in the spotlight because they – sometimes against their own will – are playing a role in the history being written in Iraq and Syria. A history in which the civilization and the natural human relationships we have come to take for granted in our civilized world, are condemned. A religion is enforced on people which propagates the return to the time of the Prophet Mohammed.

Many people in the West have reacted with a sense of disbelief. While they actively carried out a #BringBackOurGirls-Twitter campaign for the hundreds of women kidnapped by the Nigerian Muslim group Boko Haram, there was an overwhelming silence and sense of powerlessness when it comes to the fate of the women in the hands of ISIS. Stories, such as that of the American aid worker Kayla Mueller, who thanks to the testimonies of her Yazidi fellow sufferers I discovered was also held as a slave, shocked the West. And yet at the moment of writing, July 2017, thousands of women and children still remain in similar circumstances.

Extremist groups are of all times but ISIS holds the crown for institutionalizing brutal violence, inequality, fanaticism and feelings of superiority and then calling her state Islamic. This is one of the reasons why I have chosen to use the name ISIS, the name of the group declaring the caliphate in 2014. Given the fact that the little pseudo state has never been officially recognized anywhere in the world, I refuse to do that here by entitling them as Islamic State (or IS).

That is also the reason why globally various names being used when referring to ISIS. In my region, the Middle East, everyone calls it Daesh, the Arabic abbreviation for Islamic State in Iraq and Syria, ISIS in other words. The French government and media joined in doing this, especially because ISIS hates that Arabic acronym. The Americans chose ISIL, which is nearly the same, only Syria has been replaced there with Levant, the old name for the region which included Syria and Iraq.

While the BBC refers to the 'so-called' Islamic State, Dutch and Belgian media indirectly gave the terror group the recognition they so long for by referring to them as IS.

This book is not only meant to be a chronicle of women's lives under ISIS but also as a statement about what a group of fanatical men in this modern age has been doing to women, while we all stand by and watch powerlessly. It is becoming ever clearer what has happens and on a smaller scale still happens, when no intervention takes place, and the consequences of this go beyond the destruction of the lives of women. In that way a nearly irresolvable problem is created: a disengaged society of brainwashed people who also form a threat to the security of the West. Even more so, that while ISIS has lost most of her territories in Iraq and Syria, its ideology did not die. The group is still active in pockets of what used to be its caliphate, but also in other countries, like Libya, Afghanistan and Yemen. And let's not ignore that its leaders have promised that the caliphate will return.

1
THE WOMEN OF ISIS

They go out dressed in black robes, their faces hidden behind a veil with at the very most only the eyes visible. This is how we know the women from the images ISIS and their supporters distribute over the internet.

Quickly walking down the street, never alone, always in a hurry. Going out only briefly, some quick shopping and then rushing back inside. Nearly invisible for their black covering. A brief moment in the world where men rule and then back to the safe domain of the women.

These women are part of a world even more conservative than most of the societies in the Middle East – either after a conscious decision or because they had no choice. They function in a male-dominated society of which they are a part, and where they are mainly the mothers and wives of the fighters. Are they satisfied with their position in the Islamic state which was declared in the Iraqi city of Mosul in June of 2014?

What does ISIS really mean for women, I have often asked myself as I wrote for the Dutch daily *Trouw* or the Kurdish internet site *Rudaw/English*. Usually the articles were about men: training camps, military training, fighters, war, suicide bombers, kidnappings, slave traders, rapes, murders, executions.

≈ ≈ ≈

I wrote about the leadership of Abu Bakr al-Baghdadi, about the former officers from the Iraqi regime of Saddam Hussein inside ISIS, over the indoctrination and the lack of a way out from ISIS. And about the plight of the Yazidi women, who were kidnapped by the thousands with a few who had managed to escape telling me their stories.

I was curious about the other women in ISIS; the wives, the guards, the women who were already living in the region when the Yazidi women arrived in the caliphate. How did that work? Which role do these women play? How much of this role was extorted, how much voluntarily or from a sense of conviction?

The question which preoccupied my thoughts the

most, as my knowledge of the situation grew, is what their place is in surroundings which are dominated by the overtones of masculinity and testosterone? Where a religion is proclaimed in which masculinity is glorified and favors men, while for women having a family to care for is considered to be the greatest achievement. In an environment where a vision of life is being practiced which is based on something from the distant past.

It is almost impossible to fathom for us as modern people from the West. Equality between man and woman does not exist. Women play virtually no role in the day-to-day public life. Only the jobs as teachers and doctors are permitted, and then only for the benefit of girls and women. But above all, a woman is principally a housewife: she is only there for the man and the children.

That is on the outside of course, because we all know that life is never so simple, so black-and-white. A portion of ISIS' reality is invisible. In secrecy the forces of attraction, lust and sex play a big role. What you see is not what you get, as a blogger in the Syrian stronghold of ISIS in Raqqa, put it so eloquently on Twitter: *#Raqqa Belly eastern dance "Dress" its the most popular thing now in #Raqqa for the Female & Male #ISIS Foreign Fighters To buy it # Syria.*

Foreign fighters from ISIS are all beating a path to the shops to buy such a revealing set worn by belly dancers? That is quite something else than the black, loose-fitting dress with a veil.

For a housewife in the caliphate it must be just as exciting to wear such a set underneath her black dress, as it is for a Western teenager to go out in public without wearing panties underneath their skirt. And that excitement covers the man who knows about it.

But the sets can also be intended for the sex parties of the fighters with the slave girls, where they then invite a few friends over or make a video of the festivities. That is better than any Viagra pill.

And then I have reached the fact that not only the 'little blue pill' is extremely popular in the Middle-East, but also the region reigns as the biggest customer of pornography in the world.

While arranged marriages lead to much unhappiness, dissatisfaction and extramarital affairs, sex – preferably a lot and often – is enormously important, and from my observations more so than anywhere else. It is not discussed openly nor is it bragged about; as it is taboo in this culture of shame, and that is why 'if it doesn't work' one cannot visit a sexologist. The word *ayba* – something to be ashamed about, what should not be done – is already hammered into the minds of young children.

Hence the Viagra. It is often utilized in an attempt to prevent failure, and not always when there is a real necessity for it. It is a drug against the fear of failure, or some candy to make the sex even more enjoyable. Or to be able to achieve multiple orgasms.

So on the one hand you have a society where so much is forbidden, ayba; and on the other hand there is the secretive lust, the porn, the Viagra.

≈ ≈ ≈

ISIS stems from this society: from a culture of shame where everyone watches and criticizes everyone else and where it has become a sport to remain under the radar and do as you wish. A culture with a double bottom that some of those in Europe may remember from the time that religion still had an influence on the social life, and when 'what will the neighbors think?' was often heard.

The concerns how to avoid being the subject of gossip are enormous in the Middle East. Much is hidden from the outside world. Your wife is your property and that is why, also outside of the caliphate, there are a great deal of men who hide their wives away. A male guest will be given a glass of tea or a meal which has been prepared by the wife, but the spouse is nervously kept out of sight.

Houses are built to serve just this purpose, with a separate room for visitors, and in countries such as Kuwait and Saudi Arabia there are even separate male and female chambers. I remember meals sitting in the lotus position on the floor, where I as a foreign guest was permitted to dine with the men, while the women would later eat the leftovers. The rules of hospitality stipulate that guests must be well cared for. And because we come from the outside, we as Western women are allowed things that for their own wives are considered *ayba*, deviating from the norm.

Your wife, who is your property, you protect against the gazes from other men – hence the strict clothing requirements. But at the same time that which you hide and forbid is all the more desirable. The baggy dresses which are not supposed to excite anyone, lead to thoughts and fantasies – which men try to stop by sharpening the rules even further by adding even more clothing or restrictions.

This is why ISIS has added a layer of fabric three times: first came the niqaab which apart from the eyes completely covers the face, and months after the establishment of the caliphate the sitar, a veil which drapes down over the shoulders, was made mandatory. Eventually they arrived at the burqa, which is commonly used in Afghanistan but not in Iraq or Syria.

But I think this covering only leads to more feelings of desire. And frustrations. Because everything that is enticing and exciting, is forbidden. Even all the way into the bedroom.

This is not only true for ISIS. I hear stories in my area of Iraq about men who take a mistress in order to be able to experiment with various sexual positions. Not because their marriage is so bad, but because they believe that they should not do such things with their wife. That is ayba, because as the wife and (future) mother of his children she is deemed too respectable for it.

It is even the topic of discussions between young men, before the wedding night, which the girl is to enter into as a virgin of course, while the man has already had some experience. But may he then use that experience during their love making or is that disrespectful?

That you would be considering to not make use of your experience for better sex because that could be damaging to the honor of the woman – is difficult to understand. These discussions explain a great deal about the frustrations amongst both men and women. Because the sex is not about their pleasure, many women have little desire for it.

≈ ≈ ≈

Years ago, I wrote about this subject at the request of my Kurdish publisher, for a Kurdish magazine with a small circulation. I received comments such as: 'You have a lot of nerve,' but especially: 'How can you possibly know that?' Quite simply: by watching, listening, asking questions and especially thanks to local friends who were willing to share their thoughts and convictions on the subject.

And then the shops with sexy undergarments in

the Shiite neighborhood of Beirut where the women walk around equally heavily covered, or in the nice lingerie shop in Tehran, no longer surprise you.

That is why I do not believe the propaganda stories I hear from ISIS along with those from activists acting against them, about shopkeepers who are clearing their shops of all Western clothing. No one is talking about the lace strings and bras or about the pink see-through baby dolls that the men here eagerly buy for their women. Yes, that is how it works: the man chooses and buys and the women wear it. And in the caliphate it will likely be no different. And so the goods will only disappear under the counter or to a back room of the shop – and in that way the foreign fighters must have got hold of their sexy belly dancer outfits. Forbidden, and therefore most desirable.

The residents of the newly-proclaimed state are for the most part Syrians or Iraqis who were raised in a conservative culture. Their conversion to the strictest branch of Islam, the Salafism which ISIS projects, has added even more to their conservatism. Even those who had no choice but to join forces with ISIS, after it had conquered their territory, share in the conservative culture in which bared shoulders for a woman or shorts for a man are in any case deemed as improper.

It is a culture that pertains to the entire region, where kissing in public is taboo, and even at home in the presence of others. Where in a Kurdistan's second city Sulaymaniya destroyed of a kiss between a man and where a publisher in the Kurdish capi to appear before the court because of a book with reproductions of old prints from the time of the Ottoman Empire, showing men and women drinking and petting.

≈ ≈ ≈

ISIS has attracted tens of thousands of men from abroad. Fighters who have converted to the violent Salafism of Al-Qaida and ISIS, sometimes after years of fighting in Afghanistan, Chechnya or Bosnia. They have been lured by the new, exciting project of the caliphate, but also by the camaraderie of the brotherhood of fighters which they too hope to become a part of.

According to estimates made by security experts, at some stage there were 30,000 fighters from more than 100 countries. A number of these had turned against the 'loose' Western culture in which women in bikinis are flaunted on billboards. Yet another group has, after failed relationships or after years of failed flirts with women, been drawn by the prospect that the state will arrange a marriage for them to a willing Muslim girl. In an isolated case it has become known, that a Westerner who was stopped on the

...y to Syria, was attracted by the prospect of being able to marry four women.

These are men who clearly did not or could not take advantage of the freedoms offered in Western society – where relationships and sex are no longer reserved for those who are married, and where for example prostitutes are available for those who desire having multiple simultaneous sexual relationships. Or men who saw their wish to marry four women fail due to the ban on polygamy. And who, thanks to their promiscuity, have landed in one of the strictest Muslim communities in the world.

That is the assessment of the British imam Alyas Karmani, who as a young man was radicalized but has since turned his back on the Salafist Islam. He gained notoriety in Great Britain due to his resistance to the strictest form of Islam. To ITV he claimed that sexual frustration is a powerful recruitment tool for ISIS, and that young British Muslims are mainly joining for the sex. He further stated that these teens feel isolated in the 'sexualized' British society and that they are dissatisfied because their faith, culture and their parents forbid them, unlike other Western youths, from having girlfriends and intimate relationships. 'It is all about sex. These guys just want girls. That's it.'

According to the imam from Bradford, British Muslims often feel like outsiders due to the conservative and religious values of their communities in which it is not even permitted to talk about sex. 'Because if you grow up with this value that you cannot have sex before marriage, that you cannot have a girlfriend... this is something that is very haram. That is a big prohibition for an individual growing up in a sexualized society. There's a real sense of hate that you have that "I can't do this".'

What other guys can do, he means of course, and therefore envy also lies at the base of the hatred against Westerners, and ISIS happily uses it to recruit these young men.

Of course the prospect of having a slave for personal use is the source of much excitement – as is clearly visible in a You Tube video that one of the fighters shot with his phone. It shows a room full of ISIS fighters who wait giggling for the upcoming slave market, where they hope to make their move. They are mostly excited by the notion of the sex they would have with that slave, where all the frustrating rules of their conservative society would be brushed aside.

While this book is about women, I cannot ignore the men. Because they determine the margins in which these women may function. In neighboring Iran I often heard that the religious men who support the Islamic regime are in fact afraid of women – who in Iran do indeed often wear the pants. Which is why these men forced them to wear headscarves, and in doing so forced them back into their place.

I have often asked myself if that is also the case with ISIS. In a part of the territory which ISIS considered its own in Iraq, female genital circumcision (FGM) has taken place for centuries – and that stems from one of the Sunni schools of faith. A light variety, in which the clitoris is cut away, intended to remove any sexual pleasure for a woman and in doing so prevent any depraved behavior or extramarital affairs.

But also to deny her power: a woman who can give her husband what he wants in bed has influence, and she can get him to do many things. From discussions with circumcised women I know that they often have no interest in sex, because it lacks any form of pleasure for them. I believe that a lack of sexual education prevents any real change and women, but also keeps men from realizing the importance of foreplay. Women who are deemed to be too adventurous in that area are shunned, because that is not considered to be acceptable. Who had taught them this? A respectable woman is not meant to do such things!

Women can be very threatening for men who are uncertain about their position. Equal rights for women are in the regions where ISIS is active, virtually non-existent, even without any intervention by the group. Men decide whether and with whom women may marry, can have a job, or may travel.

Women may not live alone – for then they are seen as being 'available' and they will have horny men coming after them. They must marry, and should they become a widow they are expected to return with their children to their parental home.

The consequences are evident everywhere, even in politics. There are hardly any female ministers. In Iraq a quota insures that a quarter of the parliament is made up of women, but the majority of them are leashed by the constraints of their party. That is true for the majority of men as well, but from the women no initiatives are even expected. Women who present themselves as independents can expect to receive much criticism. They need to have a thick skin, since from the barrage of swear words they have spat out at them 'slut' is only one of the kinder ones.

Women are partly responsible for this themselves, unfortunately, because they are the ones raising their sons. And they treat them like princes who are denied nothing. 'While daughters must be protected and have various restrictions in place, sons learn virtually nothing about their boundaries because they always get their own way,' a Kurdish feminist justly said to me with a sigh.

That double set of morals, which allows boys and men to do everything, and girls and women nothing, determines not only the behavior of men – in a man's world where they are in power – but even more their uneasy relationship to the other gender.

And in reverse also the behavior of women.

Only in the earliest years of childhood may boys and girls play together, but quickly their worlds will be divided. For years, boys only see their female cousins and other women in the family up close. If they then go to a co-ed university, it must seem like a big candy store. But then one where you may only look, but cannot touch and certainly may not have a taste. Women are the forbidden fruit, the importance of their virginity and honor not only determines their own behavior but also how others will in turn behave towards them.

≈ ≈ ≈

If honor is so important in a society and men have not learned any limitations during their upbringing, that leads to a show of power, competitive behavior and frustrations, and due to this to (domestic) violence, sexual intimidation of women and rape. In a number of places in the Middle East women are afraid to take a taxi when alone, since the driver can molest, rape or kidnap her. Even being seen alone with a driver can damage her honor and reputation.

It typifies the society, in which the wife is nearly sacred, nearly untouchable, while men may do everything. This can only eventually lead to conflicts. And men are especially possessive when it comes to their own wife, but have few scruples in regard to the wife of another.

Many ISIS fighters have been raised in this culture, and their leaders eagerly take advantage of this. They recruit them with the promise that they may marry multiple women, and that Islam permits them to enjoy sex outside of marriage. In this the Salafists go back to a pronouncement by the Prophet Mohammed that besides their wives, men may have a slave to have sex with.

In their own glossy publication Dabiq (the publication of which has since been suspended) ISIS has explained that slavery is useful as it allows men to have sex without having to commit a sin. Because 'a man cannot be permitted to marry a free woman who is surrounded by sinful temptation.' A man needs sex, is the logic, and if you do not offer it to him he will go outside the order to have it provided. If he does not have the money to marry, or if there is no woman 'free', or in other words available within the strict rules of the faith, then he becomes a risk. Leaders who were tasked to keep their men happy and prevent possible uprisings, found a solution by offering them sex and then specifically sex in which there were no limitations pertaining to the sanctity of the wife, namely with a slave.

While sex outside of marriage is seen as a great sin, that does not pertain to sex with a concubine or slave – at least not according to the ISIS interpretation of the Quran and the life and speech of the prophet (Hadith). The ISIS bureaucracy has thought up special contracts for the purchase of a slave, in which the slave can also be sold on to someone else.

It can be compared to a temporary marriage; it can be valid for a few hours, a few months or even a few years. While this is not commonplace within the Sunni Islam, there are radical imams who will perform such a marriage. A friend from the Kurdish oil city of Kirkuk has twice had such a marriage, because he could not afford a normal wedding with an expensive feast and gold for the bride.

≈ ≈ ≈

While the autonomous Kurdish region fought against ISIS and was at the same time bearing the brunt of nearly two million refugees and internally displaced people (on top of a population of just over five million), Islamic parties in the Kurdish government appealed for the permission of temporary marriages. Their attempt to force their agenda in parliament led to much criticism in the secular forces in both politics and society. Because this was happening at a time when an ever-increasing number of Kurds were turning away from the faith following the violent interpretation of Islam by ISIS. The number of visits to the mosque had decreased by forty percent in a short period of time. More than ever before, nationalism, with the longing for self-government, is winning ground from religion amongst the Kurds.

This too has had repercussions for women; in a number of Kurdish fighting forces, after the liberation of Iraq mainly in Syria, there are hundreds of women fighting against ISIS. These female fighters believe that ISIS fighters are afraid of them because they will not be permitted to enter paradise if they are killed by a woman. At the same time these women are acting on their repulsion against the 'mental derangement' and unkindness to women by ISIS.

≈≈≈

While the Kurds turned away from faith, the battle ISIS ignited in Iraq between the Sunnis and Shiites, radicalized the latter, as ISIS portrays them as non-believers because their followers split from Sunni Islam centuries ago. This motivated thousands of young Shiites in Iraq and Iran to report as volunteers for the fight against ISIS, in order to protect their faith and their brothers in the faith. And again there is no role for women. For the Shiite militias fighting is a male-only business too.

In their fanaticism, those militias are nearly indistinguishable from ISIS; both are well-known for violent behavior, murders and decapitations. For both groups, that behavior derives from the habits and customs in the region and the double morals in regard to women, in which generations have been raised. Add to this the poverty, illiteracy, repression of groups in the population, wars and the official Islamization campaign in the nineties by Saddam Hussein, the Iraqi dictator ousted in 2003, and you will have fertile ground for the radicalized Islam of Salafist groups such as ISIS. For the Kurds, that background is not very different, but their nationalism is so strong that religious excesses remain absent.

Also in the Shiite-Iraqi society, the rights of women are under pressure. At the end of 2013, the Minister of Justice Hassan al-Shammari came with a proposed law which not only legalized marriages with nine-year-old girls, but also would permit men to have sex with their wives against their will. If women are too young or too old to satisfy their husband sexually, then he does not need to support them. Women are not permitted to travel without the permission of their husbands. The law, which after international protests was not presented to the parliament for approval, could have created a situation for Shiite women in Iraq which is not so very different from that in the caliphate of ISIS.

Besides this, Shiite militias in Bagdad play an important role in prostitution and trafficking in women. Dozens of brothels in the Iraqi capital only exist thanks to their protection. Young girls are kidnapped, imprisoned and forced into prostitution, as Rania Abouzeid describes in the October 2015 edition of *The New Yorker*. Pimps sell a kidnapped girl for between 4,000 and 5,000 dollars, (€3,420 and €4,275), and besides the militias the police also share in the profits. For the militias, sex is a source of income, where the 'rosebuds' are worth the most: the thirteen year olds cost between 300 and 400 dollars (€256 and €342) per night (with older girls and women that amounts to 84 to 168 dollars (€71 and €143). The American Ministry of Foreign Affairs concludes in its 2015 report 'Trafficking in persons', that women and children in Iraq are in increasing numbers becoming the victims of human trafficking, and then not only by gangs but also by security officers and police officers who are involved in the keeping of sex slaves.

≈≈≈

ISIS pushed women into the position of the mothers of the caliphate. They had to care for a new generation of fighters and offer the men returning home from the war, the sex they need. To ensure that their fighters would not be lacking in anything, ISIS rewarded them with a sex slave. ISIS knows all too well that in a war not only successes are booked, but that fighters must be recruited and encouraged to stay - and for this the group uses sex as a kind of 'opium for the people'.

And drugs are indeed present too: calming medication is used for example to drug unwilling women to allow the men to have their way with them, and men who must carry out a suicide attack receive drugs typically used to treat psychosis or a post-traumatic stress disorder. So it's sex, drugs and women.

And only women, because homosexuality – which does occur in the region, for instance because of the sanctity of the woman's honor - has been forbidden by ISIS. The organization throws gays from high buildings or stones them to death. Yet I cannot imagine that there are no hidden homosexual relationships, especially after it was revealed that an Islamic leader who worked with the Americans in Afghanistan, had a boy tied to his bed as his sex slave.

Women had a clear task within the caliphate. They were there first and foremost for the sex and the children, and besides this they played a limited role in the recruitment of new followers, as well as working for the morality police – as a kind of guards who maintain that women abide by the clothing rules out on the streets. These morality officers seem to have been created to help Western women accept the bitter pill that they were not permitted to fight on the frontlines.

The caliphate is a man's state, which cannot

survive without women – even though the men preferably hide them away, in the home, in backrooms or otherwise beneath several layers of black fabric. But behind the closed curtains, the unspeakable happens.

In the caliphate of Abu Bakr al-Baghdadi sex was a powerful instrument, which was needed to manage and control the violent men. Many of these men have a criminal background or a history of psychological problems. Or they are sexually frustrated. Their help was needed to create an influential state which would bring the leaders money, power and esteem.

And sex, not to be forgotten. How important that also was for the leaders is evident from the fact that they all had their own slaves. The most beautiful and young girls went to them. Yazidi girls who were witnesses to this told me that at one point the caliph Abu Bakr al-Baghdadi had at least four. His personal property, which he happily used. The Quran allows him to do so after all.

2

STOLEN, SOLD AND RAPED

At first, no one wanted to believe it: that ISIS fighters had driven into the Iraqi Yazidi villages with trucks to steal the women. That they separated the men from the women and children, and then executed the men.

There are no exact figures, but over 6,500 Yazidi men, women and children fell into the hands of ISIS; most of the men were murdered. But as still not all of the mass graves have been found and researched, their total still remains unknown.

When the Yazidis realized that ISIS had emptied entire villages, panic broke out. Thousands of families fled to the mountain which rules over their province, Sinjar. While the first people had reached the summit, fighting was still going on at the foot of the mountain. Many still fell into the hands of ISIS there.

It was August 3, 2014; a date which is not only important in the history of the Yazidi's, but also for ISIS. After the fall of Iraq's second city Mosul, two months earlier, the road was free to the fertile region around Sinjar Mountain. A strategically important area, but also a region full of 'infidels' who in the eyes of ISIS must be converted, and if not: murdered.

More important still was the fact that the conquering of the women was feeding a need in the caliphate, that ISIS-leader Al-Baghdadi had declared at the end of June. The well-known problem of every war and each army: soldiers who search for sexual pleasure following a battle, not including the 72 virgins ISIS promised them in paradise. In an effort to protect the conservative population, ISIS was in urgent need of prostitutes – even though they were considered taboo. The solution lay in the spoils of war: the 'infidel' women from Sinjar who could be used as slaves.

This is why the operation in Sinjar was so carefully planned. The Yazidi women were transported by truckloads to the caliphate. Whoever did not manage to escape ended up in schools, wedding halls and other large spaces which were used as the first shelters, where mattresses lay ready. Women and children were driven together like livestock, barely receiving any food or water. Next, the teenagers and young women were separated from the elderly and mothers with children.

Shame kept the details of that process hidden from the outside world for a long time. That the young women were forced to strip and then be examined vaginally was only revealed about ten months after the kidnappings, when a United Nations representative told Middle East Eye about this inspection. ISIS wanted to determine by this examination whether girls were still virgins, which would determine their price at the slave market.

≈ ≈ ≈

When the interview was published, I had already spoken to dozens of escaped Yazidi women, and none of them had told me this. When I tried to verify it in a conversation with an aid worker, she said she was very angry with the UN representative; this story should never have been made public. The shame was too great for the women, she said, and it would lead to problems when they returned to their communities.

I could not quite follow what she was saying, because the entire story about the stolen Yazidi women is drenched in shame and disgrace and a great deal of that is far worse than having to undergo a virginity test. It is humiliating to be graded like livestock and then to be sold, but this is only one element in the total picture of what ISIS has done to these women. And about the rest we do speak openly, so why not about this element?

After the first stories about the inspections emerged, more subsequently followed. Such as that 28-year-old Ghazala (not her real name) told to *Radio Liberty (RFE/RL)* about how ISIS fighters came to pick out their slaves. 'Every hour they came; two, three, four, five, six, seven ISIS fighters. They had large sticks and ordered us to stand up. Whoever refused was beaten.' When the selection had been made, the fighter then dragged the girl to the bathroom to 'examine' her before paying for her, she said. 'They undressed her and if she was to their liking then they bought her.'

From discussions with aid workers, I discovered that some girls were raped in the presence of other fighters and women, and sometimes by several men. They did not reveal this to me themselves, but it is also the interpretation of Yazidi artist Ammar Salim (see cadre). One of his canvasses, which portrays the takeover of Sinjar, shows ISIS fighters raping the girls on the rocky ground. When I asked him about this, he said it was based on the stories of witnesses. 'Of course I have used my artistic freedom, but the scenes on the canvas are based on the truth.'

≈ ≈ ≈

It is a common feature in all of the stories: the humiliating and violent manner in which the girls and women of the Yazidi minority were treated. Rape is a part of war, and is often not only meant as a means of humiliation. It is about much more. It is also the provocation of the winner, who has the power and therefore does as he wants. But there is often also a biological component as well: the victor wants to impregnate the women of the adversary, to be able to celebrate an even greater victory by way of generating offspring.

But the way ISIS humiliated the women is of a completely different order, due to the careful planning and organization. The theft of the women was well prepared, up to and including specially-prepared buses with tinted windows which transported the women, as well as the locations where women were temporarily housed until the need arose for a new supply of slaves.

I talked about this with Yazidi women who, after spending shorter or longer periods of time within the caliphate, had managed to escape. I have lost count, but in the years after the capture of Sinjar, I have spoken at length with dozens of women and girls. This often happened thanks to the intervention of aid workers, but the women also wanted to tell me their stories because they believed the world should know what ISIS had done to them; to let the people hear about the barbaric practices and the manner in which their people were being massacred and humiliated.

These conversations were often difficult. The traumatized women found themselves back in a world they did not know – far from their trusted village, in refugee camps, tents or in houses under construction with plastic covering the windows – where their surviving family members had fled to when ISIS came. There, they realized that a part of their family was still missing and that mothers, sisters, aunts and children were still trapped in the same misery that they themselves had managed to escape from, but also that their fathers, brothers, uncles and husbands would never be seen again because they lay in mass graves.

Most of those who spoke with me had never talked with a journalist before, if they even knew what such a person did. Many had lived in relative isolation, in villages where time had stood still and where the wave of modernization which has swept over the Kurdish cities had passed them by. Where the family was the center of their world, along with the livestock and the fields. The city life of Sinjar was years behind that of the Kurdish region. The new world entered via the television, the smart phone and the children who went to study in Erbil, Sulaymaniya or Dohuk. Many girls marry at a young age and then quickly have children.

I spoke to them with the help of aid workers and

informal translators in the camps surrounding the Kurdish city of Dohuk. It took me three hours to get there from Erbil where I live, passing only kilometers from the front line. The ride there was over roads which were riddled with holes because the war against ISIS had laid claim on the Kurdish governmental budget. That is why I allowed myself to be driven by Hoger, who works a few days a week as a security agent and guarded me like a concerned father.

And yet it was not the possible danger which made such an impression on me. It was the conversations. Sometimes, due to the distance I had to travel, I would have six on a day. The misery, often not spoken in so many words, got under my skin. It was difficult to maintain journalistic distance; the day after the interviews you could sweep me up. Transcribing the interviews meant reliving them.

I can look with journalistic distance at photos of executions, severed heads, and bodies hanging from bridges, even men in cages being drowned in a pool – all the work of ISIS. But talking to village women and teenage girls who had been used as a sex slave and whose entire life had been disrupted, did not leave me unaffected at all.

Yet much of the conversation is non-verbal or in concealing language. Sometimes the translator was a man, who due to the division between the sexes could not ask questions about rape or sexual experiences.

Sometimes the young women who worked as volunteers spoke too little English, as good female translators with the particular dialect are scarce.

I was especially touched during the conversation with a twelve-year-old Yazidi, when she started naming a list of nationalities. In that way she was making it painfully clear what she meant when she said 'many, many men' had 'bought' her.

After her escape, she found refuge in a refugee camp in Iraqi Kurdistan. She did not want to give her name, out of shame for what she had been through. I call her Smile, because despite everything she still managed to smile quite a lot.

Her sister was still in captivity together with her eight-month-old son, but like Smile, her mother was able to escape. Her father, who managed to stay out of the hands of ISIS, had no idea how to care for the two damaged women. He had to borrow money to pay doctors to treat their physical complaints, incurred by the repeated rapes.

We sat on thin mattresses on the ground in the white UNHCR tent where Smile now lived along with her parents. She was chubby and rather small. Her black hair was combed into a ponytail, and as outside spring had barely begun, she wore a black vest and red pants.

She started recounting her story the way many of the escaped women do: with the kidnapping by ISIS fighters. I have had few conversations which did not start with this; if I asked directly about their lives under ISIS, the women became confused. The first trauma always was the first topic of discussion: the fear of their escape.

Smile had fled with her family from their village of Shamal, near the city of Sinjar, towards the safety of Iraqi Kurdistan, when they were intercepted by fighters and transported out in trucks. Along the way the fighters demanded all their valuables such as jewelry, money and mobile phones. They first separated the men from the women and children, and later on the young, unmarried women from the married women and women with children. Just like with the other women, Smile was moved from building to building; sometimes she spent a night in a school or villa, sometimes a week to ten days. These were stations on the way, where she saw hundreds of other women and girls, all just as frightened as she was, and where they were beaten, snarled at and threatened, barely being fed or given water.

Next came the moment when she was separated from her older sister, the only member of her family who was still there with her baby. Smile was transferred with other girls of twelve years of age and older to the little town of Talqasser. 'My sister tried to keep me with her by saying that I was her daughter. But that didn't help.'

After they were separated, happened what she had

most feared, that she had heard the women discussing amongst themselves. Along with the other young girls, she was put up for sale for the fighters from ISIS.

I have heard differing stories about how the selection and buying process went – besides the virginity test which most likely was only carried out on the younger girls. Usually, the women were ordered to wash. Sometimes they were given clean dresses and even make-up to make themselves more attractive to the men. I heard of women who refused to wash themselves in the hope that the men would find them too dirty and would pass them by. Most of the women refused the Islamic clothing they were offered. Some of the younger girls committed suicide in the bathroom. One group of women intentionally drank a bottle of cleaning liquid one of them had found. They all became very ill, but no one died. It illuminates the sense of desperation and fear.

Often, an imam was present who ordered the girls to go with the fighter who had chosen them, and who also beat those who refused with a stick. There was chaos: women cried, screamed, resisted. Some were dragged away by their legs. They had absolutely no choice; for the ISIS fighters they were the loot, their property, slaves, or *sabiya*.

This is also how they were spoken to, as sabiya, followed by their name, as Rukmini Callimachi states, who in August of 2015 explained in *The New*

York Times in great detail how well organized the kidnapping and slave trade were. According to her, ISIS had developed a system in which women were categorized, registered and housed based upon their age. The building in which they were gathered often had a separate room where the girls could be examined by the buyers. 'When they brought us to the building, they said that we had arrived at the slave market,' a nineteen-year-old woman told the reporter.

Callimachi writes that the slave traders take pictures of the girls, to show to potential buyers. Buses filled with women were taken to Syria, and made stops along the way to 'offload' some of the women, as one woman told me. They were destined for local fighters, who had bought them from a distance.

There are price lists which have been revealed online:

A woman between the age of 40 and 50: 50,000 Iraqi dinars (€35/$42)

A woman between the age of 30 and 40: 75,000 Iraqi dinars (€54/$64)

A woman between the age of 20 and 30: 100,000 Iraqi dinars (€72/$85)

A girl between the age of 10 and 20: 150,000 Iraqi dinars (€109/$128)

A girl younger than 9 years old: 200,000 Iraqi dinars (€147/$172)

≈ ≈ ≈

In October of 2014 ISIS published an updated version of the list in Mosul, with slightly higher prices and the notation that the prices pertained to both Yazidi and Christian women. According to Christian sources in Iraq and Syria by the end of 2015 approximately 200 Christians were being held by ISIS. How many of these are women remains unknown. The pricelist from the end of 2014 made clear for the first time that they too were being treated as slaves.

Limitations were added to list stating that 'the customer may not buy more than three items'. That only pertained to the trade in Iraq, and not for customers in Turkey, Syria and the Gulf states. The new regulation was necessary due to the strong decline in the demand for 'women and livestock', according to the text. That makes no sense to me; when the new price list was published, the trade in Yazidi women was at its peak. I think that ISIS really tried to curb the prices, which rose a bit each time the women were resold, as after the preliminary euphoria about the arrival of the slave girls a lively trade had developed. Because everyone wanted to make money, with every resale the price went up again. Perhaps it was also intended to appease the flourishing wholesale trade and bring the market under the control of the state. Another explanation would be that the later list is a fake, as has been suggested by experts.

≈≈≈

The twelve-year-old Smile must have been a highly sought after purchase as a young virgin. She cost 115 Euros according to the price list. Most of the women who managed to escape are too ashamed to talk about what was paid for them. I noticed that some of them did not even know their price, because not all of the 'owners' discussed what they paid.

I also noted conflicted feelings, when the fighters who visited the house where women were being sold chose others. Another teenager I spoke to, the thirteen-year-old Zina, told me that the fighters came by every day to buy girls, but had not chosen her. She was relieved, but at the same time somewhat disappointed: 'Maybe I was not pretty enough.'

The youngest and prettiest girls were typically reserved for the leaders. But that is not what happened to Zina, nor to Smile. The latter was chosen by Salah, an Iraqi who spoke Kurdish and was from her own region. He was one of the Sunnis who had for years lived in harmony alongside the Yazidis, but had now joined forces with ISIS. Horrified Yazidis had seen how their neighbors had suddenly turned against them, and how people whom they knew from the Arabic community participated in the murders, the kidnappings and the looting.

'He took me along with another girl to the house of his sister in Mosul,' Smile said. 'He forced me to marry him.'

It took me a few interviews before I understood that there was no actual marriage ceremony in the presence of an imam, in which the women became the wife of a fighter or an emir, as those in a supervisory position were called. It became clear that for the women it was impossible to openly say that they had been raped. The term 'forced to marry' stood for 'forced to have sex'. Because they viewed the women as the spoils of war and slaves, ISIS fighters believed they had a right to have sex with them without having to be married. The bill of sale was enough, because that proved they owned them. Though it has become clear that some of the most strict religious followers did in fact still enter into a temporary marriage.

≈ ≈ ≈

The girl who was bought along with Smile by Salah, was told that they would be sold on to Saudi Arabia. I have heard this often; I think that in Saudi Arabia large sums of money were being paid for young Yazidi girls. But it is unclear to me whether they ended up there as the second, third or fourth wife, or in an illegal brothel.

Smile's companion did not wait for the trip to that unknown country where she would be permanently separated from her family and friends. She committed suicide.

For Salah, the death of a slave must have been a major financial loss. He now only had one slave left which he could sell at a profit. 'I was sold to someone in Syria, who also married me,' Smile said. And next it was her turn to be sold to Saudi Arabia. She remained for three days at a Syrian location, where she had to wait while a passport was being made for her to travel – ISIS does control parts of the borders of Iraq with Syria, but no area which borders on Saudi Arabia.

During the wait before departure, the Syrian wife of her new owner was given the order to guard her. But Smile had no desire for a life in Saudi Arabia. 'When she went to the toilet I took a knife to kill her and then myself.' The woman managed to take the knife away from her, and Smile found she had sealed her fate with the fight. 'The woman called Daesh to come and take me away. I was taken along with eight other girls to a gas factory in Deir al-Zour. There we were forced to marry.'

Instead of becoming yet another wife of a Saudi, she had ended up in a brothel in an ISIS city in Syria, and one of the worst kinds. Along with six other women, she lived in an empty shed, where they had to share a blanket and sleep on the floor. I understand from half words that the cold, wet floor left her with a serious bladder infection – an affliction which is certainly also related to the forced sex, just like all of the other injuries 'down there' for which she is still under treatment.

'No one gave me any medicine. I was beaten often. When I came outside, I was covered in wounds.' She stayed there for four months. Smile does not mention a temporary marriage, as the transfer of ownership sufficed for being allowed to have sex with a slave. And perhaps that was not even needed. From still other stories, I know that men sometimes lent out their slaves.

How many men there were, becomes evident when she starts counting: 'Men from Turkey, Germans, Italians I think, Moroccan, Tunisians, Libyans, Saudis and Africans. They treated all of us so badly…' The men repeated to the women what they had heard from the ISIS leadership: Islam allows fighters to keep infidels as slaves. 'They said that they were allowed to do this because we were non-believers, and that we had to convert,' Smile said. 'If we did not do that, they would kill us.'

≈ ≈ ≈

Converting the non-believers is of great importance to ISIS. And so, to prevent all of them from being killed, the spiritual leader of the Yazidi in Iraqi

Kurdistan released a statement in which he confirmed that everyone who had been forced to convert, would be forgiven. When the women managed to hear about this from secretive phone calls with the home front, most of them gave in to the pressure. They then had to take Quran lessons and pray five times a day.

In the brothel, Smile and the other girls were also given orders to read the Quran. 'They asked me if I could read the Quran,' she tells me with a grin on her face. 'Afraid of being beaten I said yes. Then I had to teach the other girls to read from the Quran.' She laughs out loud, because she had tricked the hated slave masters. Who apparently did not even find it necessary to check and see if Smile had actually carried out their orders.

After four months she managed to escape. 'One night there was no one from Daesh present. We ran away with six girls and hid ourselves in a house. An Arabic man was there. I was very scared, but he said: 'If you give me money, I will help you. Otherwise I will take you back to Daesh.' He asked for four thousand dollars.'

The man allowed the girls to phone with Kurdistan, where aid workers were focusing on somehow buying the freedom of Yazidi girls. In December of 2014 she was reunited with her parents.

≈ ≈ ≈

The aspect of forced conversions to Islam Smile talked about, I hear too in all of the stories. From the thirteen-year-old Zina for example, who was given shelter along with six other young women in a house of Yazidis who had managed to escape in the village of Rambucy, in the occupied region of Sinjar. 'We were given lessons in praying and had to learn the Quran from memory, all day long. They threatened and beat us. One time a cat came inside and pissed on a Quran, and then we were all beaten because they thought we had done that with their holy Quran. They fired shots just above our heads to frighten us.'

Did she remember any of the Quran texts? Zina hesitated. 'Yes, and I want to quickly forget it.'

I spoke to this teenager in the tent she had shared with her aunt since October of 2014, when after three months with ISIS, she managed to escape. She was wearing a thin headscarf loosely over her head. Her aunt listened, and sometimes added comments. She herself had managed to escape just a few weeks after being kidnapped.

Zina explained how she changed. 'I used to love school, but now I am no longer interested in it. I no longer want to study. As long as I am in Iraq, there is no normal life. I live in a hell; I want to get out of here.'

She had been seriously traumatized. That is why I did not believe her when she said that she had escaped before someone could 'marry' her. I did not question her about this, because I knew she was trying to hide her shame. ISIS considered all Yazidi women to be slaves, and the chance that the fighters would leave the women, and certainly young girls, alone was extremely unlikely. Only pregnant women and women who were no longer menstruating were off limits.

≈≈≈

This also happened to the 34-year-old Hamdiya Ali Gheshman. She was kidnapped from the Yazidi village of Kocho along with her sons Malek of thirteen, four-year-old Majed and her eight-year-old daughter Maklin. I met her shortly after her escape in April of 2015 at an aid organization in Duhok which sees to her needs, including medical care. When they took her back to the refugee camp later that day, she had bags full of clothing. And the children were very happy with the toys they had been allowed to pick out in the shop around the corner. It is the first time since the kidnapping that they had received new clothes and toys.

The little Majed was sitting in his mother's lap. Maklin was playing with a few pieces of toilet paper from a roll on the table which was a silent witness to the emotional discussions which had been taking place here. Hamdiya said that she had been bought and sold at least seven times – so often that after subsequent questions she mixed up some of the names. Each time the men returned from the front, they wanted to 'marry', she said timidly, when I ask her about this with the help of a female translator.

She wore a headscarf loosely over her dark hair. Her eyes were sunken deeply in her small face, from which the deprivation from the past nine months was clearly visible. Malek was 'missing'. After months of indoctrination in special ISIS camps and having received military training, his name was now Abu Anas and he was fighting on the frontlines – if he had not been killed.

Two months after being kidnapped, Hamdiya had been bought for the first time, by Abu Amar. He took her to Raqqa. There she was sold to Abu Tamim, who wanted to 'marry' her. She refused, she says, because her children were crying all the time. I doubt if that was reason enough not to rape her.

≈ ≈ ≈

I learned from the stories, that some men beat the women if they refused to have sex, but also that there were men who respected this. I was told that men could get their money back if the woman they had bought refused to have sex. They could trade her in for another. I do not think this happened often: it was far more lucrative to sell such a woman off to someone else. The Yazidis had in fact become nothing more than a commodity. Many fighters used their slave for a while and sold her in order to be able to afford a new one.

That was what Abu Tammin did, when he sold Hamdiya after ten days to Abu Bakr. He too wanted to 'marry' her, she said. After he had taken her children to another house, he raped her.

Abu Bakr would die on the frontline. But by that time he had already sold Hamdiya on to Abu Hassan from the Syrian village of Tabka. He was not interested in Hamdiya, but instead in her eight-year-old daughter Maklin, she told me, barely able to conceal her rage. If the sale took place according to the price list, then he would have had to pay for her separately.

From that moment on, Hamdiya fought to protect her daughter. She offered herself instead, in an effort to keep her out of the hands of the ISIS fighter. 'He said that the Prophet Mohammed was married to a seven-year-old girl, so it was okay. I refused.' The child too understood what was awaiting her. She was terrified. Hamdiya fought like a lioness to protect her daughter.

Because he did not get his way, Abu Hassan after fourteen days sold Hamdiya to Abu Salim. He took her back to Raqqa and it was there that she was separated from her eldest son Malek, whom she still had been able to contact by phone for some time.

Whether Malek was able to protect his mother and little sister in some way I do not know, but I suspect that Hamdiya had an even more difficult time after he left for the frontlines. After only two days, an unsatisfied Abu Salim sold her on to Abu Saudi – and still it was all about her daughter. Hamdiya cried and refused. She threatened with suicide if they would take Maklin away from her. 'They told me that they had the right, and that I would not be able to stop them if they wanted Majed.'

Her youngest son was only four years old. But he was not safe either, as even little boys were being indoctrinated by ISIS and prepared to be 'lions of the caliphate'.

≈≈≈

The thirty-year-old Madiha, whom I met at the same aid organization shortly after her escape in April of 2015, shared that experience. Her four-year-old daughter Maraam was also a sought-after prize for the fighters.

The girl sat on her mother's lap, clinging to her tightly. Madiha had covered her hair with a brown headscarf that accentuates her eyes, which are black pools void of any emotion. She had been bought and sold a number of times: to a young, Iraqi doctor who worked for ISIS in the hospital in Raqqa, caring for the wounded fighters and who raped her multiple times, and to a Saudi emir who beat her and tried to force her to convert. Then she ended up with Amar, a Saudi fighter. 'He was nicer than the others,' Madiha said. But despite his telling her that he would treat her as a sister, he still raped her after returning from the front.

How was he nicer then? 'He looked after my daughter, and took her to the doctor to get her skin treated.' Many children became afflicted with skin disorders during their imprisonment; ulcers and strange spots caused by a lack of hygiene. Not only Maraam had them, but also Hamdiya's children had dark spots on their faces and hands.

It soon became obvious what Amar's intentions were. He was married, but had no children. Madiha: 'He declared that Maraam would be his child, and he would raise her according to Islam. I refused: "She is my daughter and you cannot take her away from me." He said that he would release me if I would give her to him.'

Amar's father in Saudi Arabia insisted that he returned home, and would bring along the child. When Madiha had been with him for a month and a half, Amar announced he had to return to the frontline once again. After his return, the entire family would travel to Saudi Arabia, because it was becoming too dangerous in Syria with the daily American air strikes. That was the moment that Madiha decided to make every effort to escape.

But when Amar went to the front, his wife and the Yazidi slave of another fighter came to live in their house, Madiha said. One day Amar's wife left the house keys lying about. Madiha unlocked the outside door and then put back the keys so that Amar's wife would not notice. And then, in the morning when the wife went back to sleep after the morning prayers, she escaped with her daughter.

The story of Madiha's escape closely resembles that of other women. Often, they were able to escape during a moment of distraction. Sometimes, action had been taken from the safety of Kurdistan and help was sent, following a secretive phone call in which the woman was able to reveal her location. Often women had to walk for hours, hiding along the way from ISIS fighters and their supporters. Some of the route would pass through fields where ISIS had planted mines, and some escaping girls were killed or severely wounded there.

Mahida said that she wore the black dress and niqaab during her escape which she had refused to wear before. 'For no one may touch a woman wearing it.'

Hamdiya escaped with her youngest son and daughter, after she had once again been sold and ended up back in Raqqa. From there, she managed make contact with aid workers in Iraqi Kurdistan.

Some women were caught, brought back and punished. But the majority sought and subsequently received help. Some neighbors and sometimes even benevolent strangers seemed willing to help the women, often for a sturdy price due to the danger they were putting themselves into, to be caught by ISIS. The costs for this, which were paid from out of Kurdistan, in the first year after the kidnapping sometimes reached 5,000 dollars (€4,275) per person. The Yazidi women were also for them now a lucrative commodity.

≈≈≈

Many women had a problem during their escape stemming from the fact that ISIS had confiscated their cell phones, and they did not know any numbers from memory. The seventeen-year-old Perwin had, upon the persistence from an uncle, in the first days after the kidnap memorized the number of a cousin in Kurdistan. She managed to call him, after she had stolen a cell phone from an empty house.

Perwin's story shows that not everyone was being resold. The young woman had been bought by an ISIS fighter and ended up in a house in the occupied city of Sinjar, along with five other girls and their 'owners'. The original residents of this house had fled from ISIS. She remained there for four months until she managed to escape in December of 2014.

'We women cooked and cleaned, and we could talk with one another,' she said in one of the refugee camps near Duhok. Perwin caught my attention, with her open look, her thick dark hair in a ponytail and a small nose jewel. Despite the circumstances in the camp she seemed to have picked back up the pieces of her life.

She said that after her escape, she still fainted from time to time, as happened too during her stay with her 'owner' Hashem. Especially when he forced her to read from the Quran. That happened three times a day, because he wanted her to become a good Muslim.

When the fighters went to the front, one would always remain behind to watch over the women, she explained. And they were very possessive: the women were their property, and the men were only allowed to touch their own 'wife', Perwin said in response to my cautious question. 'We all had our own rooms.'

This did not mean that she was treated well. 'Hashem threatened me if I did not do what he wanted. He beat me. He was planning on selling me, but luckily I was able to escape.'

≈ ≈ ≈

Of the estimated 6,500 Yazidi women, men and children who were kidnapped in August of 2014, by April 2018 roughly 3100 women and children were still unaccounted for. Over 3000 had escaped or been liberated. Only a small number was released – in two groups with a combined total of some 400 elderly and sick. Like 45-year-old Khansi, who, together with her seven-year-old daughter Lina, in April of 2015 left the village where she had been held with hundreds of others.

I spoke to them shortly afterwards, in the meeting room of an aid organization in Duhok. They both suffer from eye problems due to their continuous crying – complaints they used to help aid in their release.

They are still in a state of shock and even burst into tears, when Khansi talks about being separated from her two eldest daughters. One of them was sold to someone in Jordan. That is a surprising fact, as it was not generally known that ISIS was also selling Yazidi women to Jordan. Although it is apparent that there are supporters there; the leader of the ISIS mother organization Al-Qaida in Iraq, Abu Musab al-Zarqawi, who was killed by the Americans in 2006, came from Jordan. Little is known about the sale of Yazidi girls to foreign countries. The women themselves have mentioned Saudi Arabia, but the trade would not solely be limited there, as became evident from the edited price list which named Turkey and the Gulf states. Under Saddam Hussein, Kurdish girls were kidnapped and taken to Egypt and Kuwait. I believe this happened with the Yazidis too: sold to all of the countries where ISIS supporters are located who are willing to pay for them.

Khansi's other daughter ended up with an emir from ISIS. He beat her so hard that she was spitting up blood and had to go to the hospital. Later on she was wounded in an American air strike while the emir was killed. Khansi knows about this because that daughter was surprisingly allowed to visit her in Mosul.

Shortly afterwards, Khansi was transferred to a village that had been deserted by its Shiite residents. ISIS had built a wall around it and was guarding it. In the village they could move around freely. Thanks to this Khansi could successfully hide her youngest daughter Lina in cupboards, under beds or in the garden when ISIS once again came to get fresh slaves. The village served as a kind of storage space for them.

Unlike Khansi, most of the Yazidi women were locked up at home. They were only allowed to leave the house if they were being sold. This often happened in special houses or, especially in the beginning, on town squares and in parks. Before leaving the house they had to put on the long, black, all-covering Islamic clothing. Most of the women I spoke to told me that they refused to wear this inside the house. They washed their own clothes at night in order to be able to wear them once again the next day. Just like the refusal to shower, this was a form of resistance which helped the women to better handle the situation, albeit ever so slightly.

≈ ≈ ≈

Zina's aunt has saved the dress she was kidnapped and escaped in, to remind herself that she did indeed make it out.

For the same reason Perwin has stuck a jewel in her nose. Most women kept the holes in their ears open with pieces of plastic after their jewelry was taken from them. Perwin wears her nose jewel with pride, as a symbol of survival, for the fact that she has left the most difficult period of her life behind her.

Painting to testify

His paintings show horrific scenes of men who are being killed and women being raped, of fighters who are choosing and buying nearly nude women. In a series of ten paintings the 31-year-old Yazidi painter Ammar Salim wants to show the world what ISIS has done to his people. 'I want to tell them about the genocide against the Yazidi's,' Salim told me, while he explained some of the paintings on the walls of his small motel room in Duhok to me.

When ISIS overtook his town of Bashiqa, he had to leave his studio and house behind. What happened to his successful business, which produced enormous cartoon figures from paper and silicone, Salim does not know.

For his paintings he combined the stories he heard from survivors with information from the media and his own fantasy.

Several buyers have shown interest in his work, but Salim is not interested. He wants to show how work to the world. 'I want the world to know what happened to us, Iraqis.'

3
THE WOMAN AND THE IDEOLOGY OF ISIS

ISIS says that its rules for women, and the manner in which they are treated, are based on Islam. But of course not the Islam of the majority of Muslims, because they have drifted away from the teachings which originated from the time of the Prophet Mohammed, according to ISIS' ideologists. For ISIS, the beginning of Islam is defining, from the time of the prophet and the first caliphs.

To make the background of this clear, I need to add something about the origins of Salafist Islam, of which ISIS is a part. That lies in Saudi Arabia, where the preacher Mohammed ibn Abdul-Wahhab travelled around in the eighteenth century to convert the Bedouin to his faith. According to him, the Quran was meant to be taken literally, and Muslims had to return to the time of Mohammed and his first followers.

He could impose that vision on the Bedouin when the local warlord Mohammed ibn Saud offered him an alliance, so that together they would be able to dominate the region which is now Saudi Arabia. That union is still in force up to the present day: currently the royal family Saud rules over the state, while the followers of Abdul-Wahhab determine the religious policies. Following the discovery of oil, they were able to spread the ideology of Wahhabism globally.

Osama bin Laden, who descended from a wealthy Saudi business family, also followed this ideology when establishing Al-Qaida. The fact that he was against the Americans and their culture, while the United States was – and still remains – the most important ally of the Saudis, and that he did not reject violence in this cause, resulted in a split, and he was eventually expelled from the country. But in their vision of Islam, Salafists from Al-Qaida and its daughter Al-Qaida in Iraq, just like its granddaughter ISIS, hardly differ from their religious father Abdul-Ahab. The differences are primarily political.

Salafists form a sect within Islam; a minority of

less than a percent of the estimated 1.6 billion Muslims. The term Salafist comes from salaf, which means predecessors or ancestors – they claim after all to base themselves on the first Muslims, the infancy of Islam.

Under Muslims, the discussion is raging about the extent to which ISIS is actually Islamic. Not even, many say, because ISIS misuses Islam. Amongst them is also the conservative strain of Salafism, which is known to be peaceful but has come under fire because of ISIS.

Yet most liberal Muslims say ISIS is indeed Islamic. They believe that everything ISIS says and does can be found in the Quran and the Hadith. But that is not Islam in which they themselves feel at home.

ISIS supporters are also known as jihadi Salafists; because of their violent interpretation of the jihad, they form a minority within a minority. Of the Salafists, the peaceful majority says that the jihad, the holy war that ISIS is waging with violence, is actually intended as a personal issue of faith a spiritual battle which leads to God.

Most Muslims believe that you may not force Islam upon someone else. But ISIS looks to the behavior of the prophet and his friends, who in their fight to establish the faith gave various groups of the population the choice to join them or be killed – and that is exactly the policy which the group is now carrying out themselves. For example, against the Yazidis: if they do not convert they are simply killed. The differences stem from the fact that the ideologies of ISIS can be described as a kind of internet version of the religion: a copy and paste Islam. They select only those Surahs (chapters) and stories about the prophet they can use to defend their own actions.

≈≈≈

What about the deal regarding women and what ISIS promises its followers? The role of the woman as a wife and mother, the use of slaves, the sex? How does all of this compare to Islamic teachings? To learn more, I consult a friend, who was at one time a Salafist himself. Clean shaven, chain smoking and whiskey drinking Jamal Husain has not been a prototypical Salafist for quite some time. He jokingly refers to it as a sin of his youth. But because he had joined the Salafists in his youth, read everything about their range of ideas and had written a number of books on the subject, he is now considered to be an expert on the subject in Iraqi Kurdistan.

I know him as a journalist from a television station in the second city of Kurdistan, Sulaymaniya, where I lived and worked for nearly five years. Sometimes he gave me a lift when I decided to walk home from work in the beautiful spring weather instead of taking a taxi. I remember that in his car we were quickly thrust in an in-depth conversation about radical Islam, in which he sometimes desperately struggled to find the right English words to answer my questions. Since he has settled into the Kurdish capital Erbil as I too have done, where he leads the youth division of Ministry of Culture, we sometimes smoke a water pipe together – although he quickly falls back to smoking his cigarettes. And now too, our discussions are often about radical Islam.

When I phone him that I want to question him about the position of women in Islam of ISIS, he tells me to bring along a translator as he deems his English to be inadequate. But when the young translator has difficulty with the complicated subject, the impatient Husain repeatedly still answers in English. The translator nearly chokes in his sweet tea when he hears Husain state that the Salafists of ISIS see women as a kind of sex machine – frank language which he can only use to me as a woman because we know one another well.

He then tries to explain that the Quran does indeed give the group the motive to do this. 'Islam is especially for men. The Quran is about the rights of men, even though the mullahs emphasize that there is a portion which was written in the name of women, the Surah for the Woman. But then you must understand that the biggest part is written in the name of the cow, and there is even a Surah for the

Infidels.' That cow intrigues me, and I search for this after our conversation. It is the second Surah in the Quran, and the longest. The title comes from the verse about Moses (Musa in the Quran) who orders his people to slaughter a cow on the authority of God. Otherwise the Surah has no other reference to any cow.

That is also true in regard to the Surah of the Woman, Husain says. Because the Quran is about and for men. The part about women pertains much more to the rights of men, rather than those of women. It states that a man may have four wives, that he may beat his wife and may have slaves. 'This verse is to show men how they must treat women.'

'The Quran says that men and women are equal, but that is not true,' Husain says. And he summarizes: the man can have four wives, the woman but one man. Men can beat women, but these do not have the right to speak against him or complain to their family about their husband. Women only get half of an inheritance compared to their brothers. The testimony from two women is deemed to be equal to that of one man.

≈ ≈ ≈

Important standard practices utilized by ISIS derive directly from the Quran. 'If you are at war and you take hostages, you may kill the men and sell or use the women,' Husain says. This rule dates from the first wars commanded by the Prophet Mohammed to establish the faith. It was then determined that prisoners of war must be considered as slaves, or be decapitated. ISIS adapted this rule to use it in Iraq and Syria for the murder of Shiite and Yazidi men and the abduction of Yazidi women.

Slavery is a recurring theme in this book, because ISIS one-sidedly reinstated it, and this especially had consequences for women. For centuries, it was part of Islamic society – the Islamic laws allowed it after all. But when international laws banned slavery, Islamic states also adhered to this although Saudi Arabia stalled up to 1964. ISIS recognizes no other laws than those of Allah, and therefore disregards all international agreements and laws, as well as those that are the result of changing times or developments.

I take a better look at an article from Dabiq, the internet magazine ISIS published on a monthly basis, as a recruitment tool but also to share information internally. In September of 2014 the article 'Before the Hour. The revival of slavery' was published, in which ISIS explains to the world what their use of slaves is based upon. The piece gives evidence of a campaign: Allah is said to have called upon ISIS to exterminate the Yazidis because they were infidels. And that should have happened centuries before, when Muslims conquered the Kurdish region. Allah will hold the Muslims accountable at the end of times that this 'infidel minority' still exists, ISIS tells the readers. If you do not want to kill the Yazidis, then you must convert them. Slavery is the seen as the perfect manner to this end. 'Many of the *mushrik* (unbelieving, JN) women and children have willingly accepted Islam and now race to practice it with evident sincerity after their exit from the darkness of *shirk* (the sin of practicing idolatry or polytheism, JN).'

For ISIS, it is an indisputable fact that Yazidis are infidels. This is why they do not have the same rights as Christians and Jews, who are seen as 'the peoples of the book' and can therefore buy protection by paying a special tax. The centuries-old monotheistic religion of the Yazidis does not belong to this, and therefore ISIS may, without consequence, use them as slaves.

Even for the distribution of the slaves, there is a reversion to the early days of the prophet. At one time a fifth of the spoils of war were for the prophet, and now that same share is for the caliphate according to ISIS – or in actuality for the leaders. The rest goes to the fighters.

In the article, the prohibition is mentioned to separate mothers and young children. And indeed: from the stories of escaped Yazidi women I was able to conclude that they were permitted to keep their youngest children with them. Although I am reminded of the heart-wrenching incident in August of 2014 in a bus in the Christian city of Qaraqosh, where ISIS sent the last, mainly elderly residents and their caregivers away. In the bus, an ISIS commander took away the three-year-old daughter of a Christian woman and threatened her with death when she protested in tears. After ISIS lost Mosul, the child was rediscovered with a Muslim family, as were also many young Yazidi children who had been separated from their mothers. In this case there was no adherence to the rules.

At the same time, the most important reason why ISIS reinstated slavery was far from religious, but extraordinarily opportunistic. The fighters had to be kept satisfied. It is used to win over new recruits, next to the promise of going to paradise, as a reward for dying for the cause. Officially, the Quran deems that by suicide there can be no entrance into heaven. This is precisely the reason why ISIS portrays the actions of suicide bombers as acts of heroism in the face of battle, and as martyrdom. For whoever kills the enemy and perishes themselves in doing so, paradise is the reward.

From tweets ISIS fighters sent, it can be concluded that the promise of the 72 virgins who would be waiting for them there, convinced many men to join forces with ISIS. The concept of the virgins in paradise comes from the Hadith, the years after his death collected details about the life and sayings of the prophet, who answered a question about this affirmatively. Nowhere in the Quran it is stated that they form a reward. Yet, according to Jamal Husain, in the Quran frequent references are made about virgins. 'And without any shame.' Freely translating Quran text to modern-day language he says: 'They are sexy women; it is about breasts and a beautiful, sexy body.'

≈≈≈

Unlike many religious Muslims, the Quran shows not the slightest sense of awkwardness about sex. So why would you then make a point of this in the worldly life? This is what ISIS bases their vision of the woman as a sex machine on, as Husain puts it. He declares that from the presumption that Allah is a man and that the book itself was received by a man and later written down by men. 'The Quran continually directs itself towards members of the same group: men.' It is no coincidence, that all of the great names in the history of Islam were also men, he added.

And if you then look for statements regarding what awaits women following death, you will find almost nothing in the Quran. Husain only managed to find one reference: if someone does good in life, the reward will come in the next life for him or her.

And that is not even solely referring to women. 'According to the Quran, the woman's role is only to serve her husband and raise their children. This is also the view of the Salafists. The women in Daesh have two duties: sex and caring for the husband and children.'

Many Islamic laws state that man and woman are not equal, according to Husain. And this goes back to the beginning, he says laughing: Adam was created as a man, Eva as a woman from his rib. In the extension of that inequality women play not a single role at the front line. Husain claims that rule by ISIS is based on a statement by the prophet. When women offered to him to go and fight in the religious wars he was leading, he answered them by saying that they must go to Kaaba, the black stone in Mecca, the center of Islam. There they could pray for victory.

But men and women are not only unequal, women are especially inferior. How much so, Husain illustrates with a reference to rules pertaining to the cleansing which is needed before prayers. 'If a baby boy pees over your hands, you may remove that with some water and go and pray. With a girl you must completely wash yourself. Girl's urine is dirty, that of boys is not. And if the faithful touch a woman after washing before prayers, then they must once again cleanse themselves.'

≈ ≈ ≈

Islam is just like Judaism and Christianity monotheistic and patriarchal. In the years after the prophet, an Islamic society was created with its own traditions, which were all equally unfriendly towards women. These assume that the woman only leaves her home twice: to marry and to die, Husain says. Stemming from those same traditions, a woman may not open the door if a man knocks. She must answer him by also knocking, because even her voice is haram for anyone other than her husband. This makes clear that the woman in Islam is not only seen as unequal and inferior, but is also the property of her husband.

In contrast to what Islamic scholars state, Husain's interpretation is that women in Saudi Arabia were better off before the introduction of Islam. 'They could write poetry, conduct business, were involved in politics. The orders for the murder of the prophet's uncle came from a woman, Hind. In this time Khadija, the wife of the prophet, could still travel alone. Now a woman may no longer do that.'

A number of other customs from the early days of the prophet which ISIS now adheres to, are a clear deterioration. Before Islam, fighters were not allowed to touch married women who had been taken prisoner, Husain explains. 'They believed this to be ayba, inappropriate, as they already had a husband.

But when after the coming of Islam, a married woman protested because the fighters wanted to treat her the same as the virgins they were able to have sex with, the followers went to the prophet for advice. He allowed them to sleep with married women. It was seen and a gift from Islam to the man.'

Husain points out that women were already treated badly before the creation of Islam, but that this did not occur in the name of a religion. 'It is now said that women were being burned at that time, but this is not written in that way in the Quran. It was mentioned that women had been burned, whereby it was said that in a next life the question would be asked out of whose name this had occurred. This is used as evidence that women were being burned before Islam. But it says nothing about it being any general occurrence.'

The question is whether the inequality between men and women originated before the beginning of the Islamic faith, Husain says. It is said that girl babies were buried in the desert at the time. '"Do not kill the boys due to poverty," the Quran says. This means in any case that before Islam children were being killed for that reason.' And not only the girls; the prophet especially wanted to spare the boys.

≈ ≈ ≈

Back to ISIS, and the manner in which they choose what they wish to use from the Quran and the tradition of the life of the prophet. I go to see another friend, Kawa Mahmoud, a Kurdish communist who studied theology in the Netherlands – where he closely examined Islam too. It seems like an odd combination, which in fact tells us something about his sense of curiosity and openness. Due to his prominent position in the Communist Party, he held the position of Minister of Culture in the Kurdish government between 2008 and 2014.

Mahmoud, whose wife has led a Kurdish women's organization, played an important role to get legislation for the protection of women introduced. In 2011, the Kurdish parliament unanimously passed a law partly thanks to his efforts, which forbids female circumcision and also intends to fight domestic violence – a law which is unique to the region.

I visit him at the Communist party's offices in Erbil, where he is the deputy secretary general. Outside, pigeons noisily search for shadow from the heat just outside the high windows of his office. We drink tea, and talk about his recent stroke and the speech problems, which have mostly disappeared following treatment in the Netherlands.

He tells me that he sees ISIS mainly as a pragmatic group. 'The group changes her strategies and tactics in order to reach her goal: the acquisition of the power. And only because she has an Islamic state, Islam is seen as the solution for everything, for all of the problems in society. ISIS has taken what it can use from various Salafistic groups and models, and is the most violent of all of those groups.'

This pragmatism can be seen in the treatment of women. Although women belong at home, with their family, ISIS would have no hesitation in calling on women to go and vote if that was deemed necessary, Mahmoud says. 'In order to control the active women, they try to organize them, as with the Khansa brigade.' That brigade controls whether the rules pertaining to clothing are observed in the caliphate, and is entirely made up of women.

An example is also the exception that ISIS makes on the commandment for women to stay at home: they are permitted to work as doctors or teachers. 'They want to build a society, and are in need of teachers to give lessons in Islamic education. For female students they need female teachers,' according to Mahmoud. Without female doctors there would be no health care for women, and sick women would be unable to bear children or care for their families.

Mahmoud points to what radical Islam bases the balance of power between man and woman: 'There is a statement from the prophet which says that if the man is angry with his wife, she will not be able to enter paradise but will instead enter hell.'

≈≈≈

Pragmatism is also the base for the reintroduction of slavery, Mahmoud believes. While Shiites know a marriage of pleasure, a temporary marriage for the sex – the *sighe* or *muta'a* – this does not exist in the strict Sunni convictions. 'Some fundamentalist groups even consider the muta'a to be a sin. However, sex with slaves is allowed, because they are seen as infidels, which is also the reason why slaves may be kept.' This is precisely why ISIS' ideologues have created their own form of a marriage of pleasure, Mahmoud says: 'The *jihad al-nikah*, a sexual jihad. It is a type of marriage, but one without the involvement of an imam.' Western women are said to have been recruited with this concept.

≈≈≈

An Iraqi-Kurdish ISIS fighter, who at the beginning of 2014 managed to escape, revealed in a conversation with the site *Your Middle East* inside information about the group. 'There are Muslim women, who freely offer their bodies to the jihadists. This is called jihad al-nikah, and according to ISIS they will be rewarded for this in heaven. These women were usually with the commanders, I did not see them with the normal jihadi fighters.' He also says that he and his comrades were promised women, in heaven and on earth. 'They told us that all female prisoners who were not Muslims would be our wives, and that this is what Allah wants.'

As an ISIS fighter, he was continuously presented with the rules. 'In an Islamic holy war, you may not in any case kill the women and children of the enemy. They may only be taken prisoner. Sexual intercourse is permitted with the female prisoners, even if the jihadists are already married. You may buy and sell these women, but the children you must raise to work in the home or to become jihadists.' One takes part in this because he has no choice in the matter, he says 'because ISIS openly and proudly proclaims carrying out these deeds as the implementation of the Sharia'. Rape is for that reason justified too, according to ISIS: 'Supporters believe that you may even sleep with female prisoners against their will, if they are infidels, non-Muslims or apostates. This happened with Christian women in Raqqa after their husbands had been publicly executed, and I have witnessed this.'

≈≈≈

Kawa Mahmoud points out that with ISIS, the implementation sometimes, and certainly in this case, goes against the rules of Islam. Muslims may marry Christians, 'because a Muslim may have a

Christian wife. Christians after all belong to the peoples of the book. If ISIS then takes them as slaves, it is in direct conflict with her own faith.'

For Christians and Jews, the Prophet Mohammed makes an explicit exemption – partially because Islam is based upon (the books of) these religions. If they payed taxes, they therefore enjoyed protection and were able to live in the Muslim community.

But that is not the reality of the caliphate, as becomes clear from the story of the same escaped jihadist, who worked as a technician and repaired radios. He recounts how in a Christian home in Raqqa he found six jihadists demanding sex from a Christian woman and her teenage daughter. 'I told them that Islam prohibits to force women, and that children are not to be touched under any circumstance.' When they then threatened him, he went to an ISIS court to be proven right. 'The judge said that I was wrong because a thirteen-year-old girl is no longer a child, in essence because the Prophet Mohammed and his wife Aisha married when she was only nine years old.'

ISIS fighters used the example of Aisha time and again when Yazidi women tried in vain to protect their young daughters. Aisha is said to have married the prophet when she was only six but the marriage was not consummated until she was nine. This is why the ages ISIS fighters use differ greatly, with some claiming that a girl of seven is already suitable for sex.

More explicitly, young girls are declared suitable for sex in a pamphlet ISIS published at the end of 2014: 'Questions and answers about the taking of prisoners and slaves.' Here it noted that it is 'permissible to have intercourse with the female slave who hasn't reached puberty if she is fit for intercourse; however, if she is not fit for intercourse, then it is enough to enjoy her without intercourse'

I wonder what it is that makes a girl fit for sex, but that is not mentioned in the pamphlet. That apparently depends on the interpretation of the person involved. Even worse is the fact that no age limit is mentioned, which means that all of the young girls ISIS has taken prisoner are in fact at their mercy.

At the beginning of the pamphlet it states that the sabiya is a woman who was brought by Muslims from *ahl al harb*, the peoples they are at war with. Her imprisonment is simply allowed because she is an infidel.

This is true too for having sex with her. That is permitted for the new owner 'immediately after taking possession of her' if she is a virgin, and otherwise 'her uterus must [first] be purified'. How that must be done is not mentioned, but I suspect that she must first have had her period.

The pamphlet gives explicit permission to also keep Christian women as slaves: "There is no dispute among the scholars that it is permissible to capture unbelieving women (..) such as the *kitabiyat* and polytheists'. The first category are the peoples of the book which Mahmoud mentioned and to which the Christians belong – whom ISIS names as infidels, in conflict with Islam. I consider this to be a typical example of the pragmatism of ISIS. We need women, let's not be difficult about it and just use every woman who rejects us, the leaders must have thought. For Shiite women – fellow Muslims whom ISIS views as infidels – may also be kept as slaves according to the pamphlet.

It makes interesting reading, because it reveals that the manner in which the fighters of ISIS deal with the captured women is indeed based upon something, but also because it becomes clear that those rules are just as easily ignored. For example, the requirements for dealing with a slave. She may be beaten to punish her, but no bones may be broken, her face must be spared, she may not be tortured and not beaten solely for the enjoyment of the person involved. This rule too is often ignored, as I have heard from the stories from Yazidi women who were severely beaten – sometimes because they were caught trying to escape. 'A male or female slave's running away [from their master] is among the gravest of sins...' the pamphlet states. And here I see evidence that ISIS is making her own rules, separately from the Quran and the Hadith: there is no punishment for this in the Sharia laws, the unknown writer of the pamphlet admits, 'however, she is [to be] reprimanded [in such a way that] deters others like her from escaping'.

ISIS fighters also violate the rules regarding the reselling of slaves, just as those pertaining to loaning out a slave to others for the sex. The latter is not allowed, although according to escaped Yazidi women, it happens continuously. Only the owner may derive pleasure from her, the pamphlet states.

≈≈≈

For a number of the ISIS fighters raping a slave became a sort of religious experience, as became apparent from an article by Rukmini Callimachi in *The New York Times*, 'ISIS Enshrines a Theology of Rape', in August of 2015. In the piece she allows two teenage Yazidi girls to tell their story. The fifteen-year-old of the two protested against an Iraqi ISIS fighter in his twenties who raped her. 'He kept saying that it was *ibadah*,' she says; he used a word from the Quran which means worship. 'He said that raping me was his prayer to God. I told him: "What you are doing to me is wrong, and it will bring you no closer to God." And he said: "No, it is allowed, it is halal."'

The other girl, twelve years old, says that every time before an ISIS fighter raped her, he said that he was not committing any sin. Because she adhered to another faith than Islam, the Quran gave him the right to rape her – the faith allowed and encouraged it. 'I kept telling him that it hurt – please stop.'

Both before and after the rape the ISIS fighter dropped to his knees in prayer. 'He told me that according to Islam he was allowed to rape an infidel. That by raping me, he came closer to God.'

Perhaps that religious experience is caused by the conviction of many within ISIS, that the Yazidis are not simply infidels, but devil worshippers. In their religion Malik Taus is an important figure: a fallen angel who after paying penance was taken back by God, after which he became the peacock king, one of the seven angels in the Yazidi faith. For them, the existence of both good and evil alongside one another was essential; the devil exists next to God (see frame). One ISIS leader explained that he therefore could do everything with her he wanted, one of the girls told Callimachi. 'He said to us that Malik Taus was not God. He said that Malik Taus was the devil, and "because you honor the devil you are our property. We can sell you and do with you what we want."'

≈ ≈ ≈

The American reporter mentions yet another rule ISIS enforces. The group asks all of the women about the exact date of their last menstruation, to make certain that they are not pregnant. According to the Sharia, a man may not have sex with a slave if she is pregnant or has reached menopause.

That the women for many ISIS supporters form a step towards heaven, is also clear from a line in the ISIS pamphlet stating that whoever releases their slave will be rewarded in paradise. There is even a special document created for this purpose, which Callimachi was able to get hold of because an escaped woman had brought it along. The Lebanese 'owner' of this 25-year-old Yazidi woman had given it to her because he was going to blow himself up in an upcoming attack. It is a 'document of emancipation', signed by an ISIS judge, which frees her. Every ISIS checkpoint to which the young woman presented it to along the way through Syria and back to the Kurdish region in Iraq, accepted it without hesitation.

≈≈≈

How ISIS connects slaves and religion became obvious from the special Quran reciting contest which ISIS had organized during the Ramadan of 2015 for her fighters in Syria. Yazidi girls were the main prizes. The first three prizes for reciting a number of Surahs from memory were a sabiya, a slave, and for the fourth to tenth place a cash prize. I could not believe it at first: a 'slave' being given for memorizing a few Surahs? But the announcement made via Twitter seemed real. A few of the Surahs which the fighters had to recite are amongst the most violent in the Quran. It may be that ISIS wanted to show that her fighters were indeed religious Muslims – something the outside world disputes. And that the Islamic education functions, and therefore so does the caliphate. And perhaps it is just a thumbing of the noses to all of the criticism: ISIS is not affected by the criticism and simply continues on down its path.

The criticism partly derives from the fact that politically ISIS stems from a secular movement: Saddam Hussein's Baath party. In that framework, Mahmoud points out that ISIS' decisions are not only given from a religious standpoint. The influence of former members of the Baath party on the organization is substantial. ISIS is the summation of Saddam's high-ranking officials, soldiers and security officers, along with radical Muslims. The latter had been partly brought to Iraq by Saddam to fight against the Americans, for when and if they would invade the country – which they did at the beginning of 2003. The battle was continued by Al-Qaida in Iraq, the predecessor of ISIS, in which former loyalists from Saddam's Baath party worked alongside Islamic fighters from all over the world. Saddam recruited a special force for this: the Fedayeen Saddam, tough men completely dressed in black which remind me of the current ISIS fighters. They too were well trained in commando and guerrilla techniques. The Fedayeen were originally created by one of Saddam's sons in 1995 as a personal militia, but in 2003 they formed a professional commando unit of some 30,000 to 40,000 members, all predominantly Sunnis.

In April of 2003, when I was in the southern Iraqi city of Basra shortly after the American invasion, I discovered a place where these Rambo's had delivered a fierce battle with the Americans. At a man-made lake, I still found bulletproof vests and balaclavas lying about between the shrapnel and spent bullet shells. They had fought here to death. Later I heard that they had also been deployed in the oil city Kirkuk; there too a part of the Fedayeen-brigade had fought to death. Fedayeen means: they who offer themselves.

That is also what is expected from the ISIS fighters, with the promise of paradise, if they take the enemy with them into death. It is a fact that Saddam's soldiers were involved in the battle and that they were responsible for the strategies which were being followed in doing this. It is also known that after the American invasion, the Fedayeen joined the – mostly Islamic – resistance in Iraq. Everything suggests that the Fedayeen from that time have since been training ISIS fighters.

But wasn't the Baath party secular and socialist,

with close ties to Moscow, I put to Kawa Mahmoud. What is there between former Baathists and Salafism? Religion was always a part of the party, he says: 'The Baath party said in the beginning that it wanted a form of socialism with also space for religion and the Arabic culture of the region.' Yet initially secularism was the dominant factor. 'Women also played a role in the party.'

But the world was changing and the Baath party had to make adjustments. 'When Baath came into power, there was a different political balance in the world than later on. It was the Cold War, and there was an aspiration for Arabic unity. After the rise of the Islamic Republic in Iran, the balance changed.'

Religion was becoming ever more important, he concludes. In the years following the Kuwait war which he lost, Saddam in 1993 began with a campaign of Islamification, as a part of attempts to win over the population that was becoming ever poorer and therefore also more religious.

Just as ISIS now, Baathists were extremely pragmatic. 'Saddam decided to have a religious resurgence.' Islamic groups were given more freedom, the study of the Quran became part of the educational curriculum, and Saddam even spoke of forming a Pan-Islamic state. Ideologically he was borrowing an ever-increasing amount from the Muslim Brotherhood. 'Actually, Saddam has planted the seeds for ISIS'.

When the Americans arrested Baath party-members after 2003, for their part in the planning and execution of attacks, they ended up in prison along with Iraqi and foreign Salafists. The fusion that took place there, led to ISIS and the current caliphate. Secular supporters were also given a role, at least according to American army reports, as during a number of raids targeting high-placed Iraqi ISIS leaders not a Quran was found.

≈≈≈

On many fronts ISIS is not particularly original; much has been copied from other extremist Islamic groups. This is also true for the way the group uses the end of times for its battle. According to the revelation, the final battle will take place in the village of Dabiq – hence the name of the ISIS magazine that was published for a couple of years. In the last battle, the Muslims will defeat the Christians. The return of an Islamic caliphate forms the prelude to the battle, and thus to the end of times. Men – but also women – are promised that they may take part in this, and therefore when the time comes they will be on the right side.

'All fundamentalist groups think the same about it,' Mahmoud concludes. 'There are also Christian sects which are preparing for this. But that in itself is not the problem. It is, when ISIS is gaining power to force us to think just like them.'

On lists of characteristics of sects, many elements of ISIS can be found. For example, the manner it brainwashes and indoctrinates its supporters, where the ambitions of the leader, Caliph Baghdadi play a major role. But also the way members are led to believe that they have been chosen to take part in a special project.

At the same time, a mutual language is of importance, and this is evident among the foreign recruits who mix ISIS-Arabic with their own language. Due to this, a kind of ISIS-speak has developed – as with George Orwell's 1984, a book which could easily have been written about the ISIS state. And I know that Saddam was a huge fan of Stalin, who must have inspired Orwell in writing this book about a totalitarian state.

≈≈≈

Over ten years ago, I conducted an extensive research about a political sect, the Iranian resistance group Mujahedeen Khalq (MKO). I now conclude that the parallels with ISIS are numerous. Especially similar is the way members are brainwashed and made totally dependent on the organization.

In both organizations sex is used to manipulate supporters. In MKO, married couples were forced to separate, after which all relationships and sex were forbidden because all love and affection had to go to the leader. That led to the creation of a group of frustrated people who were even willing to die for their leader. ISIS uses sex in the religious discourse, so supporters of the group are willing to fight and die for them.

Women are important for both groups. In MKO, they are officially placed above the men. In their total obedience to the leadership they are instrumental in the oppression of the members. ISIS also uses women to control members. By offering sex to fighters and officials, but also through the wives who play an active role in the organization and the enforcement of the slavery.

Another component of the sect culture is the way a group shuts its supporters off from the outside world. For ISIS, this means that when you end up in the caliphate, the chance that you will ever make it out alive is slim. That is true as well for the Yazidi women, and for the women who were recruited as jihadi brides. There is no room for doubt; whoever dares to voice any criticism or attempts to escape, pays with their life.

Falling away from faith is not allowed or possible – ISIS uses this not only to prevent its own members from turning against the group, but also to turn them against the Shiites. Because they have been deemed as apostates. Apostasy is a serious transgression in Islam which is punishable by death, and for ISIS this is true to the extreme.

The Shiite majority in Iraq and Iran form a minority in Islam of approximately 15 percent. The difference with the Sunnis in essence derives from the choice of the leadership of Islam, and originates soon after the death of the prophet. The Sunnis wanted to choose his successors based on their knowledge and experience, the Shiites saw the descendants of the prophet as the designated candidates.

The two groups have been fighting about this since the sixth century, with current-day Iran, Iraq and Syria as their historical battleground.

≈≈≈

Violence is an essential part of the history of the region. This is apparent in the way ISIS utilizes violence to sow fear – both for its supporters as well as for the outside world. This has been copied from Saddam's regime. Even his political ambitions for an Arabic unity and later on an Islamic union state, emerged again with ISIS in the way it wants to extend its caliphate outside of the Middle East.

Ask Jamal Husain what we can learn from history, and he answers cynically: 'That no one ever learns from it'. But to me, it is mainly that Islamic groups like ISIS use Islam to justify their battles, while in reality it is all about sex, money and power – and hardly about religion. Power for the caliph and his assistants, and money to guarantee their future, no matter what happens.

We know that ISIS made a lot of money from the sale of oil, antiquities and even hostages, and that the population in the ISIS-occupied territories has not gained a cent from this: on the contrary, ISIS drained them financially by imposing one tax after another. It would be interesting to know just how much money ISIS leaders have been able to slip into foreign bank accounts. In Iraq, under the former Shiite premier Maliki at least 26 billion dollars (22.9 billion Euros) of the government budget is confirmed to be missing, and just like everyone in Iraq I expect that it has found its way into Swiss bank accounts or shady companies on the Cayman Islands.

Fighters and officials of ISIS are given salaries and bonuses with a marriage or move, but I am convinced that a large portion of the incomes have been skimmed off for the leaders. As a nest egg, if the project of the caliphate does not in fact succeed, and they are deposed or eventually chased out by a world power – as has been the case since the fall of Mosul in 2017.

That it happened, was not due to the way ISIS treats women, nor to the many other countless human rights violations, such as the use of children in the battle and the decapitations. Or because of the repression and the enforced ideology on so many civilians. It happened because of the balance of power in the region, which made another solution imperative for Syria and Iraq, in which an Islamic caliphate no longer fits. And that has little connection to women, religion and ideology.

Yazidis and their peacock king

Yazidis, who are also known as Ezidis, are considered to be the original Kurds, who populated the region when the first followers of Islam came in the seventh century to bring their religion by the sword. In the subsequent time, they have been persecuted often for holding onto their faith; Yazidis maintain a list of 73 serious attacks on the religious group before the arrival of ISIS. Among the perpetrators are many (Sunni) Kurds, and although the Kurdish government emphasizes the historical ties, the Yazidis in Iraqi Kurdistan have been discriminated against and persecuted for centuries. They live mainly in the Iraqi province of Sinjar and the area surrounding Duhok, and their numbers are estimated at 650,000, of which 100,000 reside in the West.

Yazidis follow a centuries-old monotheistic religion, which is related to Zoroastrianism and the ancient faiths of Mesopotamia. It also has aspects which can be traced back to the Torah and the Bible. The elements (earth, air, water, light) play an important role. The sun is pictured on monuments with the beams pointing downwards, and there are prayers at sunrise and sunset.

Yazidis believe that God has created the earth and then given the control of it to seven angels, which are led by a fallen angel God took back after his penance. This Malek Taus, the peacock king, is mistakenly associated with the devil, which has led many Muslims to consider Yazidis as devil worshippers. According to Yazidi mythology, they descend from Adam, but not from Eve, and to maintain purity marrying outside of the own faith is forbidden.

Yazidis go on a yearly pilgrimage to their temple in Lalesh, located a half-hour's drive from Duhok. Here Malek Taus is said to have landed to give the earth his color and its nature. The temple contains the grave of their spiritual leader from the twelfth century, Sheik Adi ibn Musafir. Yazidis are strict about cleanliness and are divided according to a strict caste system, with the Baba Sheik as their spiritual leader, comparable to the pope for Catholics, and a prince (mir) as a political leader. Both belong to the highest caste.

4
WOMAN AGAINST WOMAN

Your husband brings home a slave. It is something I cannot even begin to imagine. Many fighters already had a wife – they lived in the area which ISIS conquered or they came from the outside and had their spouse come over after a while, or they married a Western recruit. And those Iraqi, Syrian and also foreign wives were confronted with a new woman in their home. She was dirty, cries and put up a fight.

From a Western explanation of women's solidarity, you would suspect the wife to care for the poor, kidnapped, raped girl. Nothing is further from the truth. From the stories of escaped Yazidi women,

I can only conclude that the women were just as involved in the slave 'circus' as their men. Although they could object on so many levels, in reality they rarely did or do. This tells us something about the powerlessness of these women, but also about the fear for the husband and his fists. It is partially an inheritance from the many wars the region has known, because wars are known to lead to more domestic violence. Many men cannot deal with their traumatic experiences and take them home.

Part of the Western women, but also the other foreign women have been brainwashed to such an extent during the ISIS recruiting process, that they find slavery to be normal. This leads to women even defending extremely women unfriendly policies. One of them is a so-called Umm Sumayyah al-Muhajirah, who offered her opinion in the ninth edition of Dabiq. Using the catching headline 'Slaves or prostitutes' this foreign woman, who came to the caliphate as a jihadi bride, argues in favor of slavery. She claims that rape and prostitution are not an issue, as what is happening has been approved by the Prophet Mohammed. Reports of sexual abuse by ISIS fighters derive from 'devious and wicked slave-girls' who 'made up lies, and wrote false stories'.

She tries to discredit the many witness accounts of escaped Yazidi girls, probably because those stories about rape and violence are damaging to the recruitment of fresh followers from the West. She writes that Yazidi women who have converted to Islam are well treated and are welcome in the families of the fighters. Many had willingly given up their religion. It is a claim that greatly distorts the reality; not a single Yazidi converted to Islam without being forced to do so. Most who did, did so because they simply did not want to be murdered.

Umm Sumayyah's article is, just like the rest of Dabiq, in English, and I would guess that it is her mother tongue. In line with the established ISIS-speak, she scatters her flowery language with Arabic words. Umm Sumayyah is thrilled about the arrival of the slaves. 'I and those with me at home prostrated to Allah in gratitude on the day the first slave-girl entered our home,' she writes. 'Yes, we thanked our Lord for having let us live to the day we saw *kufr* (disbelievers, JN) humiliated and its banner destroyed.' The word banner means 'flag' here, and conjures up the association with the black ISIS flag which the group places everywhere.

A world of despair could be hidden behind these words. Of a jihadi bride who came to the caliphate only to be married off to a man she shares nothing with and who may even treat her badly.

The article in the internet magazine is especially intended to show foreigners that Islam allows slavery. Umm Sumayyah claims that the Prophet Mohammed told his men that following a victory on the battlefield they should kill off the enemy fighters and make slaves of their women. According to her, it is good practice for the Moslem community to follow this example. Normally it is forbidden for a man to approach a woman, but that ban does not apply when the woman is his slave, she says. A man who is unable to find a suitable wife, but can find a slave, indemnifies himself from fornication.

As Umm Sumayyah continuously repeats how glorious the actions of ISIS are, she evokes the impression that she is also trying to convince herself of this, or that she does not entirely believe it or is merely repeating what she has learned. She names examples from Islamic history like Abraham who took Hajar as his concubine who gave him his son Ismael, and the Prophet Mohammed who had a son, Ibrahim, with the Coptic maid Mariyah who was as his concubine. Yet she must have realized that this comparison is not valid since these women were not kidnapped and overwhelmed like the Yazidi women. She presents these comparisons to announce the fact that Yazidi girls have also become pregnant, and that a number of them have been released after having converted to Islam.

≈ ≈ ≈

I was able to conclude that this is true based on the stories from escaped Yazidi women. If they convert – complete with a testimony from an imam – after a ten-week period, they will no longer be a slave. They are permitted to go outside, for example to visit a mosque. But they must marry and may not leave the caliphate.

Yazidi girls have indeed become pregnant, with a number of them managing to escape. But given the large amount of raping going on it is surprising that only a small percentage seems to have become pregnant. Some believe that they were given a contraceptive injection, which I find to be a rather strange contradiction with the strides of ISIS to create as many new little lion cubs as possible. One explanation could be that sex with pregnant slaves is forbidden, and since the women are first and foremost there to have sex, a pregnancy would have to be prevented.

The article shows at the same time, that the introduction of slaves took some of the faithful in the caliphate by surprise, and that not only Muslims from outside the caliphate are objecting to this. Which is a thorn in the side of Umm Sumayyah. She speaks of 'false rumours' that al-sabi (the taking of prisoners during the war) is a sexual offence, and that tasarrī (keeping a slave as a concubine) is considered to be rape. 'If only we'd heard these falsehoods from the kuffar who are ignorant of our religion. Instead we hear it from those associated with our Ummah, those whose names are Muhammad, Ibrahim, and 'Ali' she writes with indignation.

She reproaches the manner in which some ISIS supporters have defended their state, following criticism from 'the kafir media' about the slavery: 'as if the soldiers of the Khilafah had committed a mistake or evil.'

Umm Sumayyah declares that she is full of pride. 'I write this while the letters drip of pride. Yes, [...] we have indeed raided and captured the *kafirah* women (unbeliever women, JN) and drove them like sheep by the edge of the sword. All glory belongs to Allah, His Messenger and the believers, but the hypocrites do not know.'

ISIS was merely the executer of Allah's will, she claims: 'We did not humiliate them, but it was Allah who did so at the hands of His truthful slaves who did not wish for anything except for Allah's word to be supreme and the *kuffar's* (unbeliever's, JN) words to be the lowest. Their aim is sublimity for the religion and humiliation of whoever desires a religion other than Islam.'

Fiery words from someone who is either a religious maniac, or an austere believer or merely faking this. At the same time, she is the wife of a fighter who brought in a Yazidi slave. Even if she is as happy about this as she claims, I find it hard to believe that this does not also lead to jealousy. That is in any case what I have been told by the escaped Yazidi women.

In those stories, I hear a great deal of powerlessness. What can you do if your husband brings home such a slave? The man is the one in charge, and you must obey him. He can divorce you without any problem: simply calling out 'I renounce you' three times is sufficient.

Clearly protest is not an option, nor is showing any signs of humanity. It is often the wives who treat the Yazidi women the worst. Some will do this to avoid being punished by their husbands, for some jealousy plays a role, while others are simply convinced that Islam permits them to do so.

≈≈≈

Often, the fighters burden their wives with guarding their 'slaves'. Any faith in the solidarity of women disappears, when you hear with just how much fervor they are committed to their task. Smile told me for example about the wife of the Syrian who wanted to sell her to Saudi Arabia: 'If she locked me up, she gave me only water. If I cried, she beat me.'

Hamdiya also ended up with a married fighter, Abu Bakr. His wife also gave her barely any food. She was only given the scraps. When Abu Bakr was at the front line, his wife would lock her up in a room. She was only permitted to see her children sporadically when he was home. 'She called me an infidel and said that I should be grateful.'

The Yazidi women had to clean the house, and sometimes cook. But they were not permitted to eat with the family.

When Mahida's daughter had to go to the hospital, she was not allowed to go along because of the risk of escape. She told me how Arabic women tried to convince her that she could earn her freedom. 'They said: "To have freedom like us, you must read the Quran. That will take two years, but after that you will be given your freedom."'

These are relatively nice women. But Zina, who said that no one was nice to her, and that the wives helped their husbands to abuse the Yazidi women, was not the only one. The women focused their aggression on the Yazidis, as if they are dogs you just kick – since dogs are seen as being unclean in the Middle East and are therefore mistreated. 'If I had not managed to escape, I would have preferred death,' Zina said.

Eighteen-year-old Manar lived for two months in the Syrian town Manbij with a 38-year-old Chechen fighter, whose 25-year-old wife was jealous of the young slave girl. When he was killed, the two women were at each other's mercy, she said. Then her misery really started. 'She hated me.' The young Chechen wife cut Manar's long, black hair to a short boy's cut. After two months, she sold her to another Chechen, but he then took her to the prison where she was initially locked up with prostitutes. She spent more than three months with Syrian women in a cell, as the only Yazidi. Why, she does not know, but she thinks it was the revenge from the Chechen wife.

One of the kidnapped Yazidi women had with her the five-year-old child of her brother. To prevent being separated from him, she pretended that the child was her own. She talked about how the boy was abused by the wife of her 'owner'. Scratches and bruises supported her story. It bothered the wife that the poor child, who had not yet even been to school, did not speak Arabic, but only a Kurdish dialect.

≈≈≈

To prevent any mutual solidarity, ISIS used a number of the women as police women, in a special unit which was intended to make sure that women out in the streets were abiding by the rules: they should be completely covered, not wearing high heels and accompanied by a male family member. That is the Khansa brigade, which was largely made up of foreign women and operated in both Raqqa and Mosul. Violation of the clothing rules resulted in forty lashes from the cane, and whoever tried to escape from the caliphate was given sixty, according to two young women who had gone to Syria to marry a fighter there. After their escape to Turkey they talked to foreign journalists about their role in the brigade. From their testimony, it became evident just how much pressure the women were under. They had gone into hiding, because they were still fearful for the wrath of ISIS.

'What upset me most was lashing old women when they weren't wearing the proper clothes,' the twenty-year-old calling herself Dua told the press in Turkey. All women had to adhere to the clothing rules. 'Those women were like my mother.'

But in fact these two policewomen were themselves also victims. Both had lost their husbands in the battle. The older of the two, who called herself Umm Ous, was forced into having a new husband, an Egyptian militant, who abandoned her when he decided to escape from ISIS.

The Khansa brigade made the news thanks to the actions of a few British ISIS women who had posted photos of themselves on Twitter, dressed in a black burqa and holding machine guns. They said that they handed out beatings, ordered executions and ran the brothels where the Yazidi girls were being held as sex slaves.

And yet in Smile's account not a single woman was mentioned, not even as a guard of the brothel in Syria where she ended up. Perhaps because the Khansa brigade was not active in Deir al-Zour? Or because there were probably both official and informal brothels. And Smile was presumably in the latter type.

At the same time, there are stories of a woman known as Umm Zeineb who was active in all parts of the caliphate, of whom I assume that she was member of the Khansa brigade. She is said to have selected the Yazidi girls for the fighters, and would beat them if they refused to have sex. According to a young woman who ended up in her hands three times, she cursed at the women she punished, poured hot water over their hands and beat them with plastic cables.

One of the escaped women told an aid worker how she and two others, after such a session, had come up with a plan to kill her. The guard had to call for the help of a Chechen fighter to be rescued.

The brigade also punished Yazidi women who attempted to escape. One of them still managed to flee on another occasion, and therefore lived to tell her story. After her third failed attempt, her face was shoved into a container filled with hot water and hot oil. Her skin was so badly burned that she was nearly unrecognizable.

≈≈≈

British women were in particular active in Khansa, and often had the lead there. Of the woman who was said to have lead the brigade in Raqqa and was named as Umm Hanza in various international media, the nationality is unknown, but she showed sadistic pleasure in measuring out punishments, and carried not only an AK47 but also a pistol, a knife and a whip - so she could give anyone the correct punishment at any time.

The brigade was housed in hospitals and schools, strategically positioned throughout the cities. In Mosul the armed women in black patrolled in groups during their shifts which began at four in the afternoon and finished around seven in the evening.

Yazidi women were confronted with the Khansa brigade as soon as they arrived in the caliphate. In Mosul these were the women who checked to make sure that they had not secretly hidden away money or jewelry, or even a telephone. It was also these Khansa women who had to determine whether the Yazidi girls were still virgins.

Even if some might have been more enthusiastic than others, all these women share, together with the wives of the fighters, emirs and leaders, responsibility for what happened to the Yazidi girls and women.

≈ ≈ ≈

Gender advisor from UNAMI, the United Nation's Mission in Iraq, Idah Muema sighed in frustration when I talked to her about this problem. 'No one wants to discuss the female offenders', she said. She had difficulty getting the issue into the spotlight, partially because there is little information about the level of participation of women in the sexual violence against other women in the caliphate. 'We need to do research. Only then will we be able to determine which measures we can take and how we can prevent it.'

I understand that the women saw the Yazidis as animals, just like their men do. And in the best case scenario, as infidels without any status. But I wonder if they knew anything about the variety of the sexual acts their husbands were performing with the women and girls. Surely they could not have been completely unaware of this. Perhaps they simply did not want to know, or were happy that they were not the victim. That it happened is certain. Yazidi girls have told me about this, still in shock about the acts they had to perform, and full of shame about the perversity. I am convinced that many men were inspired by the porn movies that are so popular in the region, and therefore did everything with their 'slaves' that they dared not do with their own wives. Trios, gang rapes, using sex toys, oral and anal sex, sadistic sex – and so much more.

The UN worker mentioned in chapter 2, also exposed the story of a Yazidi woman who had been set on fire because she refused to take part in performing a perverse fantasy. That punishment is even in violation of the rules listed in the ISIS pamphlet regarding the treatment of slaves.

As most of the victims are from the conservative farmlands, they barely had any education or any knowledge about the society outside of their Yazidi villages. They must have been completely overwhelmed by the sexual nightmare they ended up in. A society in which such things can happen without punishment, and even worse, where this type of behavior is institutionalized, offers women no protection whatsoever.

Many ISIS women must certainly have realized that the presence of the Yazidi women protected them from the violence which was becoming ever more nestled in the society. By offering the fighters slaves, ISIS in fact was damming up domestic violence, because the men could take out their frustrations mainly on the Yazidi women.

≈ ≈ ≈

And yet despite all of this, friendships also developed. I discovered this from the story of the 42-year-old Khanu. Along with her two sons, Farhad of fourteen and seven-year-old Sarhad, she was taken to Raqqa, where the 75-year-old Afghan doctor Abdulrahman took her into his house. When he bought her, he already had three wives, who were housed at three different locations.

When he was not working in his clinic in Raqqa, the doctor would go to the frontline to treat the wounded. Given the enormous shortage of doctors in the country at war, his status was nearly untouchable. His income was clearly enough to afford having three wives and a slave.

Khanu had to clean the house and cook. The rest of the time she spent locked in a room. After the purchase, it was obvious that he would be having sex with her – even though Abdulrahman already had three wives. 'He treated me badly, was always angry, never gave us enough to eat. We were always hungry,' Khanu recounted in the bare, unfinished house of her brother-in-law in the Kurdish Yazidi village of Khanke where she was staying since her escape.

Khanu's sons lived with her, except when they had to go to the special indoctrination camps, or, like Farhad, to military training and later on to the frontline.

Abdulrahman tried to convert her and her sons, and he forced them to pray five times a day – as was customary in the house where she lived with one of his wives. The woman treated her fairly, in comparison to her husband, and also her daughter, Khanu says. But she did not intervene when they were beating her. 'The daughter, who had a small child, forced me to do the housekeeping, called me slave and servant, and said I only had to obey.'

But Khanu had some luck too. Abdulrahman also had a Syrian wife, and she, unlike the others, was nice to her. She had married the Afghan after her first husband, a Syrian fighter from Aleppo, had been killed – a new marriage, arranged by ISIS as is done for all war widows who are to marry again. As all women in the caliphate are supposed to be married.

The Syrian woman watched in revulsion how Khanu was treated. According to Khanu, she even pushed Abdulrahman to act with more humanity. 'But he said that we were infidels and had to be treated this way. After that she divorced him.' That was an extraordinary act; normally it is the men who cast off their wives for whatever reason. It was likely not an easy task, as she would have had to convince a judge. It is of course possible too that Abdulrahman treated her just as badly and that she therefore wanted to be rid of him.

Khanu had clamped onto the Syrian, her being the only woman who treated her as an equal. After her divorce, they remained in contact. When Khanu eventually saw an opportunity to escape with her sons after having been resold twice, the woman even gave her shelter in the nearby town where she lived since her divorce. 'We remained there for five days,' Khanu told me. From there she phoned her brother-in-law in Khanke, and he arranged for someone to be waiting at the Turkish border to help her, once she had crossed. But the Turkish border guards initially did not allow the three of them to enter. Only after the third attempt to pass the border, and after paying

1,500 dollars (€1,282), they were granted entry into Turkey.

According to Khanu, the Syrian also tried to get away but she was unable to pass the border. 'She was very poor.' Khanu was unable to help her. She had to not only look after herself, but after her sons too. Therefore, the contact between the two victims of ISIS, who had forged an exceptional friendship in a country where the arrival of ISIS has completely distorted human relationships, was lost.

Other minorities also kidnapped

Yazidi women make up the largest group that was kidnapped by ISIS, but there are also kidnapped Christian and Turkmen women in the caliphate. They were taken from Mosul and the surrounding areas, and from their villages in Syria. Their numbers remain unknown, because their communities have not advertised it much.

In mid-2015, the number of missing Christians was estimated to be at least 200. The group of the Turkmen is comprised of both Sunnis as Shiites, and while many Sunnis joined forces with ISIS, Shiites were kidnapped, murdered or driven out. Of them, at least a hundred people were missing in September 2015. The Shabak, a small, ethnically religious group in Iraq with a centuries-old faith, encountered the same fate. An estimated 180 people are still missing. The number of women involved is unknown, but given the fact that anyone who does not agree with ISIS's interpretation of Islam is deemed to be infidel, the chances are, that just like the Yazidis they are treated as slaves.

It is known that ISIS kidnapped a number of young women from the Christian city of Qaraqosh; their fate is unknown. There is only one unconfirmed story about a Christian woman who had been raped so many times as a sex slave that she had a mental breakdown, after which ISIS is said to have dropped her in Iraqi Kurdistan. Older, Christian hostages, who had been taken in Syria and released due to illness, said that men and women were held prisoner separately in overcrowded rooms, with virtually no hygiene and with little food or water. Ransoms of a 100.000 dollars a person were demanded, and a number of small groups of both men and women have been released. After the liberation of most of Iraq from ISIS, a number of Christians have been found, mostly elderly people. How many are still missing in 2018, is not clear.

5

BAGHDADI'S BRIDE

If fighters get slave girls, the leaders will also share in that treat. So the prettiest girls will go to the big boss, I have often thought. And who would be good enough for Abu Bakr al-Baghdadi?

I stumbled across the answer to that question by chance. The story begins for me on a dark night in May of 2015, when American commandos raided a house at a Syrian location near Deir al-Zour, in search of an ISIS leader who later turned out to be an important link for the sale of oil and other goods. Abu Sayyaf, as was his alias, was killed in the operation but his wife survived and was taken prisoner.

In keeping with the ISIS habits, she called herself Umm Sayyaf. 'Abu' and 'Umm' are Arabic for 'father of' and 'mother of', and normally this would be followed by the name of the oldest child. But with ISIS even childless young men are also called 'Abu' and that is why a random name is often stuck onto this. 'Sayyaf' means executioner, and I seriously doubt that the couple has a son named Sayyaf.

Abu Sayyaf was a Tunisian who had joined ISIS, judging from the name used by the Americans: Faith Ben Awn Ben Jedi Mural al-Tunisia. If he was so important that an American commando team was sent to get him, why did he die during the operation? And who is his wife really?

After the operation, the American army reported that the Sayyaf couple was in the possession of a Yazidi slave, who was rescued during the operation. This confirmed that not only fighters but also leaders had slaves in their homes.

A few days after the operation, the American magazine Foreign Policy wrote on its website that in October of 2014 a Yazidi slave had managed to escape from Abu Sayyaf, and that she had been held along with a kidnapped American aid worker, the 26-year-old Kayla Mueller. The role Umm Sayyaf played in the interrogation and torture of the American was subject to an investigation, according to Foreign Policy.

Kayla Mueller was kidnapped by unknown assailants and handed over to ISIS in August of 2013, during a demonstration outside a hospital run by Doctors Without Borders (MSF-Spain) in the Syrian city of Aleppo. Her Syrian boyfriend, who was helping Doctors Without Borders to restore their internet connection, was released soon after, but Mueller remained imprisoned for eighteen months. Her identity remained secret at the request of her family and was only revealed after her death.

≈≈≈

When I read all this in May of 2015, I remember a conversation I had with a Yazidi family in one of the many white tents of a refugee camp in the Kurdistan Region of Iraq. It had gotten snowed under by testimonies that had seemed more relevant for my investigation into the women in the caliphate.

The family has been hit hard by ISIS. While we talk in the tent about their escape, the wedding pictures are brought out. Jameel Gheddo, who is the head of the family, gives me a list of family members who have been kidnapped, 24 in all, and a list of eighteen family members of whom he knows they have been killed.

Shortly after their abductions, Gheddo has been in brief contact with five of the women in Mosul – in the beginning ISIS allowed some of the girls and women to keep their phones so that their stories to the home front would feed into the fear of the organization.

One of the five women is taken to Raqqa, where

she cooked and cleaned for ISIS. About two other young women they know, that they were with ISIS fighters in the Syrian city of Shadadiya, including the fifteen-year-old Suaad. She was there together with two American girls who had been kidnapped by ISIS, the family says. 'That was what another Yazidi girl who had escaped told us.'

At that moment in the tent, I cannot imagine which American 'girls' could be in the hands of ISIS. In the assumption that there must have been some mistake in the translation, I forget about the incident.

≈ ≈ ≈

But about a week or so later, I read on the site of Foreign Policy that Kayla Mueller passed up a chance to escape from Abu Sayyaf with a Yazidi girl, because the other foreign woman being held was too weak to come along. She let the girl leave alone. I then realize that this must be the very girl who reported to the family I spoke to, about how their daughter Suaad was doing. As all escaped Yazidis, she reported to family members about the location of their loved ones.

The girl's name is Sozan, Suaad's Uncle Jameel Gheedo tells me, when I visit him again in the camp to try and get answers to the many questions I have regarding the new facts I have discovered. He tells me that he is a taxi driver, and that at the time of the abductions he was on a trip to Kurdistan. This is why he survived, and can now conduct the search for his family members.

It seems that he brought Sozan in contact with American security officers in neighboring Duhok, who were most interested to hear her story. This has eventually led to the commando action six months later, which unfortunately did not lead to the release of his niece Suaad.

So was it intended to free the American women? But who were they? Gheddo has written down their names, but when he finally finds the bit of paper in between all of the papers in his pockets, he can barely read his own handwriting. Kayla he can make out, but that other name? 'Karol?' he says hesitantly.

In February of 2015, following eighteen months of imprisonment, Kayla Mueller was killed, according to ISIS in an airstrike by American coalition planes. More than six months before, in July of 2014, a commando action to free her had failed, because she had been moved two days earlier – perhaps ISIS had received a tipoff. American media reported that she had likely been given as a slave to a high-ranking ISIS commander, or was forced to marry him. That could have been Abu Sayyaf.

≈ ≈ ≈

Thanks to Jameel Gheddo I find the fourteen-year-old Sozan and then most of the pieces of the puzzle fall into place.

The girl is surprisingly young, and even looks quite childish, when I meet her in the company of two sisters and an uncle. I had not realized that she was just a teenager, and the fact that she has managed to hold on to that childishness despite having been held captive by ISIS for three months, astonishes me even more. She wears her long, brown hair in a braid, and dons a pink blouse and black pants.

On a bench in the shade of a teahouse in Duhok which is closed for the Ramadan, she and her sixteen-year-old sister Dalal talk about their three months with ISIS, and about their recent attempts to get a passport, so that they can join a group of traumatized Yazidi girls who will be receiving treatment in Germany.

Along with Dalal, Suaad and two other Yazidi girls – all fourteen and fifteen years old – she first ended up in a prison where the two American women were also held, Sozan says. From there, they were taken together with Kayla to a house in the Syrian city Shadadiya, to Abu Sayyaf. Sozan calls her Kayla Karol, which explains the name on Gheddo's paper. Later on, I realize that this confirms the authenticity of Sozan's story, because Kayla's father is named Carl. And in the Arab world, the name of the father is used as a last name, hence Kayla Carl – which in Arabic sounds like Karol. Sozan cannot have known this from anyone but Kayla herself.

The second American, who she knows as Luisa, remained behind. She is old, Sozan said, and was complaining about her entire body hurting. Later on, I learn from a reliable source that this woman is not an American, but most probably European. Her family has never officially made public the fact that she is in the hands of ISIS, and in 2018, her faith still is not known.

≈≈≈

The Yazidi girls could communicate with Kayla because she spoke a basic Arabic. Sozan thinks that she had learned this during her long imprisonment by ISIS. A good relationship developed, in which Kayla repeatedly stood up for the girls and prevented them from being beaten, which resulted in her getting into trouble herself, Sozan says with visible affection.

They asked her again and again to come with them when they were planning an escape, but Kayla refused. She would as an American draw too much attention, whenever they would have to ask for the help of civilians along the way, she gave as the reason, and would be putting the girls in danger.

Along with two others, Suaad made an escape attempt, but they were caught. She received 'a very severe beating' but was surprisingly enough returned to Sozan and the others afterwards.

Other women who escaped were punished much more severely. What was so special about Suaad? I only understand this, when Sozan tells me who she was 'married' to: the big boss himself. Suaad was the Yazidi slave of Abu Bakr al-Baghdadi.

And what about Kayla, I want to know. Is it true that she was the slave of the Tunisian Abu Sayyaf?

Sozan can't stop herself laughing about this. 'No, she was with Abu Bakr al-Baghdadi.'

The big ISIS leader himself? She too? Sozan says that she had seen him frequently at Abu Sayyaf's place. 'He was there often. I do not know why. But every time he took Kayla away. And then later on, she would come back to us.'

Abu Sayyaf would pick up Kayla in order to bring her to Baghdadi, who had his own room in that house and stayed there on a regular basis. And when she would return to their room, she would tell the girls each time, often in tears, that he had 'forced her to marry him,' Sozan says. Because of their shared fate, the five women had bonded greatly.

≈ ≈ ≈

Kayla Mueller was repeatedly raped by Baghdadi. She was not only his prisoner, but also his slave – ISIS after all permitted keeping Christian slaves.

Yet Sozan's little sister Dalal has the impression that there was even a marriage. 'He said to Kayla that if she refused to marry him, he would decapitate her,' she says. When Kayla after a visit to Baghdadi returned to their room, she was crying. She said: 'he raped me and made me his wife.'

According to Dalal, he gave Kayla a Quran and she was receiving lessons every day. She was apparently being forced to convert to Islam. Moreover, she had to wear black, concealing clothing, so that the other men in the house could not see her. This does seem to indicate that he considered her to be his wife. Dalal says that she was even given an expensive watch as a wedding gift.

Does this then explain why the multiple attempts by her family to get her released failed, because she was the wife of the caliph?

That she was not simply given to an ISIS fighter but instead to the highest boss himself, does not really surprise me. Firstly, it is a matter of status: Mueller was an ISIS showpiece, as an American she naturally had a higher status than the other slaves Moreover, Baghdadi could taunt the Americans who were on his heels with this: he had seized one of their own.

This can also explain the air strike which is said to have claimed her life in February of 2015. I suspect that it was aimed at Baghdadi, because the Americans had discovered that Kayla Mueller was his slave. But he escaped.

ISIS accredited the attack to Jordanian jets, as part of a series of coalition attacks in retaliation to the horrific death of a crashed Jordanian pilot a few days before, who was burned alive by ISIS.

The Americans originally doubted the story, until the family of Kayla Mueller received an email with three photos of the dead body of their daughter; ISIS declared when announcing her death, that 'our sister' had been killed.

Shortly afterwards, in March of 2015, Baghdadi himself narrowly survived an attack on a convoy, in which he was so badly injured, that he had to give up the daily leadership of the caliphate.

≈ ≈ ≈

Kayla and the four girls formed a special group for ISIS. They all belonged to the ISIS leadership, Sozan tells me. Fifteen-year-old Inaz was 'married' to Abu Sayyaf. Elsewhere in the house were Jamila and Ahlam, the latter being with Abu Tamim who was responsible for the supply of new Yazidi slaves. But whom she and her sister Dalal were 'married' to, Sozan does not say, she feels too ashamed to. Talking about others is easier.

The two sisters are the only witnesses and sources for this story, but I have no reason to doubt their words. Virtually no one knows about a second female

Western hostage in the hands of ISIS. In a second conversation with supplemental questions, Sozan's answers remain consistent.

I contact the American Ministry of Foreign Affairs for a confirmation. It sends me on to the federal intelligence service, the FBI, who to my amazement phones me via an open line in Erbil with the request not to name the second hostage. The service then informs me that they have no comment and directs me to the White House.

≈ ≈ ≈

Meanwhile the spokesperson for the Mueller family, Emily Lenzner, surprisingly contacts me. She confirms the story. The family only recently had discovered that Kayla was 'the property' of Baghdadi. She wants to dispel the rumors that Kayla had remained by ISIS of her own free will. That was not true, Lenzner emphasized: 'It was a torture'.

That impression is thanks to a letter Kayla wrote to her parents in the spring of 2014, which they made public following her death in 2015. In this she said that she was 'totally unharmed and healthy' and has been treated 'with the utmost respect and kindness'. Besides this, she asks her parents not to negotiate for her release, because 'I never wanted to burden you with this'.

We discuss the air strike in which Mueller is said

to have perished. There is much doubt whether the version publicized by ISIS following her death was true. She deems my theory worthy of consideration, that the bomb was intended for Baghdadi, who could have visited Mueller earlier. The family is attempting to discover what exactly happened to their daughter in the last eighteen months of her life. They too have many unanswered questions about her death.

The White House eventually comes, by way of the spokesperson Alistair Baskey, with a rather vague reaction: 'At this time we are not able to confirm a cause of death. The U.S. military has indicated there was no evidence of civilians in the target area prior to any Coalition airstrikes at that time. What we are certain of is that ISIL is responsible for Kayla's captivity and death.'

Shortly afterwards an American governmental official, of whom I was not given any name, emails me the following official statement: 'The target struck on February 6th by the Royal Jordanian Air Force, with the support of U.S. Military aircrews, was a known ISIL weapons storage compound located near Raqqa, Syria. This target had been struck on previous occasions and was damaged. It is not uncommon for the coalition to conduct multiple strikes on the same target.'

The details surrounding the death of Kayla Mueller remain a mystery. But thanks to Sozan's account, other important pieces of the puzzle have fallen into place. For example, about the house belonging to Abu Sayyaf where Mueller and Sozan were being held, together with the other Yazidi girls.

≈ ≈ ≈

When I ask Sozan, how they got through their days, she tells me that she and her roommates did the housekeeping and cooked. In great amounts, because 'besides the leaders there were many more Yazidi women in the house, whom we were not allowed to talk to', Sozan says. It was clear that it was not intended that they would be able to share information with others about their relationship with the leaders and the activities in the house.

I get the impression of a brothel intended for the ISIS leadership, which also served as some kind of distribution place for the slaves, especially the youngest and prettiest. 'Umm Sayyaf has sent many Yazidis to Daesh', Sozan says. Umm Sayyaf must have been a good source for the Americans; she knew everything about the slaves and the hostages of ISIS, Sozan tells me.

She hates the woman, whom she describes as being in her thirties. But in reality she is only 25, I know from American sources. The young Iraqi woman was a very convincing accomplice in the crimes against the Yezidi women. 'She was very bad for us. If we did not understand something, she would tell Abu Sayyaf that we had misbehaved, and we were then beaten.'

Umm Sayyaf, whose name is actually Nasrin Assad Ibrahim, was transferred by the Americans to the Kurdish authorities in Iraq, a few months after the commando action. They have since charged her with conspiracy in the death Kayla Mueller. Prosecutors say Umm Sayyaf had kept her captive, allowing her to be repeatedly raped by ISIS chief Abu Bakr al-Baghdadi. This was very unusual at the time, given the fact that then not a single ISIS fighter arrested by the Kurds had been brought to justice.

'We will always be relentless in our efforts to identify, locate and arrest those who are responsible for the kidnappings and murders of American citizens,' said the FBI's Assistant Director in Charge, Paul Abbate to the BBC.

Sozan and her younger sister Dalal eventually manage to escape from the regime of this woman. On October 8th of 2014, at one o'clock at night, they make a successful escape attempt. The date and time are etched into her memory, Sozan says. She is happy to be back with their third sister, who was not kidnapped. 'But my father is still with Daesh, just like my brothers Mirza and Seif', she weeps. The chance is huge that they are no longer alive, but she will not mention that.

She does not know what after her departure happened to the Yazidi women she had to leave behind. From American sources, I know that they were moved, after which Mueller was separated from the rest. Abu Sayyaf had found a new location for his transit home for slaves, which also served as a meeting place for the ISIS leadership.

That is why it took until May for the Americans to undertake any action; they were not able to immediately determine where, in the area around Deir al-Zour, his new hiding place was located. The action by the commandos was probably intended to arrest the Sayyaf couple, in the hope of gathering information about the remaining Western hostage. If this was successful, we do not know, but it is known that on the computers and flash drives seized by the Americans, a wealth of information was found pertaining to the structure of the organization and the finances of ISIS, as well as about the organization of oil pumping and trade.

≈≈≈

When I go once again to visit with Jameel Gheddo, to ask for news about his niece Suaad, he has surprising information. During the past months, he has used his network to try and find family members. Through Arabic acquaintances and mediators, he has succeeded in gaining the release of no less than sixteen of them from ISIS, after buying them back. Amongst them are women with three children, and young girls.

Gheddo has spent thousands of dollars, money which he received from Kurdish organizations and other funds which he borrowed – even though the financers know that he will never be able to pay them back. In the meantime, his quest is keeping him busy full-time (and by mid-2018, he had secured the return of all but six of his original list of 24). Because of this, he also knows that Suaad and her fourteen-year-old sister are still in the hands of ISIS. He received a remarkable sign of life of Suaad: a picture of her and two other Yazidi girls.

I sat and stared at it for a long time. There are three girls in the picture, in black dresses, with black hijabs, the niqaab that normally would cover the mouth and nose has been folded back and lies on the top of their heads. They are holding a bouquet of fake flowers. Suaad shows a forbidden bit of bare leg with a chequered sock. What stands out, is that all three are smiling – and that their eyes are too. Judging from the relaxed manner that they are posing for the picture, I believe that they must know the photographer. Has he or she said something funny? Compared to the many emaciated women that I have seen after returning from ISIS, they look remarkably healthy.

Jameel Gheddo says that he ended up with the photo because the girls have been put up for sale. It is a sort of contact advertisement, which reached the

Yazidi's in Kurdistan via Arabic intermediaries. Since he received the photo via an aid organization, Gheddo has been searching in vain for the person who sent it digitally out into the world. He raises his hands desperately towards heaven. Suaad seems so close, but no one in his network can help him any further. Every time I see him in the next years, he tells me the search still goes on. Until mid-2018, when he tells me Suaad has been located in a village near Raqqa. She had been in contact with her mother over WhatsApp. Gheddo has offered the ISIS fighter holding her money, as he did to dozens of others holding family members. "But he doesn't want to sell her," he says, not able to hide his disappointment that this time, he fails to secure the return of a dear one.

≈ ≈ ≈

The story of Sozan and Suaad offers me a new insight into the lives of the Yazidi women in the caliphate. I can only conclude that not everyone is treated equally badly. Not everyone is starved, and mutual friendships are helping the Yazidi women to survive.

But I also conclude, that the manner in which the women are being sold has entered a new phase. Other families who are looking for their women, tell me they had also received photographs, which had been placed on the internal internet network of ISIS, where the fighters were able to choose and buy a slave.

≈ ≈ ≈

Thanks to Rukmini Callimachi from The New York Times, I discover how this trade works. She spoke with a Yazidi businessman, who had acted as a buyer of a slave. He discovered that the traffickers make portrait photos of the girls and women, in which they are shown sitting in an empty room, emotionlessly looking into the lens. They are presented to the buyer as Sabiya 1, Sabiya 2, and so on. But that type of naming is missing from the photo with Suaad. It is also extraordinary because it shows three women, who are posing naturally without visible coercion.

When I show this photo to Sozan, she recognizes Suaad immediately. She chuckles a little. She never wore a hijab or abaya inside the house. 'Only when they took us outside, to take us somewhere'. Suaad does not know the other two girls in the picture.

Because of the fact that the two women in the photograph with Suaad have no connection to the Yazidi women at the Sayyaf's place, we now know for sure that the group of slaves of the leaders has been split up. What has happened to the other girls there were in their room is unknown; Sozan has not yet been able to see them again in freedom.

≈ ≈ ≈

I offer the parents of Kayla Mueller to make the contact between them and Sozan and Dalal, as they are still looking to complete the puzzle of what happened to their daughter in the caliphate. They consider the offer, and many months later decide to accept. A year after I found out about Kayla Mueller's fate as Baghdadi's slave and wife, they meet up with Sozan in Germany, where she is now living.

During emotional hours they share stories and shed tears for the pain inflicted. The parents are told that Kayla was as a mother as well as a big sister for the Yezidi girls that were imprisoned with her. As the Yezidi aid worker who was present later told me: 'She was like an angel, who cared for the other prisoners.'

6

MOTHERS OF THE CALIPHATE

What nearly all the women in the caliphate have in common, is the fact that they first and foremost are seen as mothers, whether they are the wife or widow of a fighter, a jihadi bride, married to a leader, or a maid. Only the slaves have a different status; they are primarily there for the pleasure of the men.

Women in the caliphate are the mothers of the next generation. And not only for the leaders or the fighters, but also in their own eyes; they are proud to be able to contribute to the future of the caliphate. That is also how the women in the West have been recruited: to bear children – the so-called cubs of the state – and in doing so making a contribution to the caliphate.

Most of the foreign women only discover after

their arrival in Syria, how the society they will be part of is organized. For those who are with ISIS, it is a kind of socialist utopia, inoculated with religion. That is evident from a report by the press agency The Associated Press (AP), which gives an impression of the daily life in Raqqa. For three years, from 2012 onwards, AP spoke via social media to Abu Bilal al-Homsi, a 28-year-old Syrian fighter from Homs, who often informed the foreign media about the battle against President Assad. He had fought for a number of years alongside resistance groups in Homs.

≈ ≈ ≈

In 2014 Abu Bilal joins forces with ISIS. He meets his Tunisian wife through social media. At the time of the siege on Homs by the Syrian army in 2011, she was already following him there. Once he has joined ISIS, he contacts her by Skype. She tells him that her brother has joined the group in Deir al-Zour. In keeping with the customs of the region, Abu Bilal asks the brother for her hand, as the representative of her father who is in Tunisia. Then, the 24-year-old women travels via Algeria to Turkey, and on to Raqqa, along with other women who are on their way to join ISIS. There she is given shelter in a guest house for single women in the headquarters of the Khansa brigade. Single women are to marry as quickly as possible to prevent their honor being endangered.

According to a member of the internet group Raqqa is being slaughtered silently, who operates under the alias Abu Ibrahim al-Raqqawi, the guest house is a luxurious place with air conditioning, beautiful furniture and a garden, to bridge for the newcomers the transition from a luxurious life outside.

To marry his Tunisian wife, Abu Bilal makes the risky trip from Homs to Raqqa, right through the middle of a war zone. In Raqqa the elite of ISIS lives, predominately made up of foreign fighters and their wives, coming from Europe, Asia, America and of course the Arab world, just like Abu Bilal's new wife.

From the beginning of the caliphate in June of 2014, Baghdadi has not only called upon fighters to join them, but also on doctors, engineers and administrators for the institutions of the new state. The number of women belonging to this elite class is estimated to be one to every ten men who immigrate to the caliphate; if there are approximately 40.000 foreign fighters (the latest number for 2018), there will be some 4,000 foreign women. The uneven numbers once again emphasize the need to kidnap the Yazidi women, and the habit of then selling them on.

Next to the foreign fighters the elite is formed by Iraqis, mainly former Baath members. They live in the luxurious houses and apartments which were previously the property of the Syrian regime. And Yazidi women have ended up with them too, often having been given as a gift by those of the lower ranks who wanted to get on a good foot with the leadership.

ISIS takes good care of the foreigners: they are given a car and petrol, and health care is free for them while normal citizens and fighters must pay for it. For the children of the English-speaking fighters a special English-language day care facility has been opened, despite the fact that English is seen as the language of the enemy. English teachers for a while were unable to find work in the caliphate, until the leadership realized that it was the language uniting many of its foreign recruits.

For the elite, there are touristic bus trips through the caliphate. From social media it seems the women are the ones taking the most advantage of this.

Unlike in many other places under the control of ISIS, the supermarkets in Raqqa are well stocked with luxury products like Nutella, chocolate bars and energy drinks, but also the latest smart phones. There are many internet cafes and the elite also have internet at home. Media activist Al-Raqqawi therefore refers to Raqqa as 'the New York of the caliphate'.

Essential for ISIS is to help fighters who want to marry. After all, mainly single men travel to the caliphate. No wonder that ISIS, after taking over

Mosul in June of 2014, immediately opened an Islamic court in the city. Not only for the enforcement of Sharia laws, but especially to perform marriages according to the regulations of ISIS. The contract for this is drawn up by the judges of that court. Normally ISIS rewards such a marriage with a premium of 500 dollars (€427). The reward given to Abu Bilal and his bride is three times higher: they received 1,500 dollars (€1,282) so they could decorate their new home and go on honeymoon. Because Abu Bilal's wife is not only a future mother, but also a doctor who speaks four languages, she is an important acquisition, since in health care, men and women are treated separately. And also because male physicians may no longer treat women, there is now a shortage of female doctors.

Following a short honeymoon which they spend in Raqqa, the young couple settles in Homs. A premium of 400 dollars (€342) awaits them for each baby, on top of the monthly salary of 100 dollars (€86). Abu Bilal is also given an army uniform, clothing, cleaning supplies and food. He furthermore expects ISIS to care for his family when he is at the frontline: 'Because when a fighter is on the frontline, how can he bring home food?'

After the marriage, Bilal's wife calls herself Umm Bilal. It is expected that she abides by the strict rules in the caliphate. ISIS published a manifest for the recruitment of Arabic women, that has been circulating in Arabic on jihadi websites and was composed by the Khansa brigade. The British think tank Quilliam translated it, thus allowing others a glimpse into the lives of women in the caliphate.

The basic idea of the manuscript is that a woman's life should be based at home, caring for her husband and the family. Ideally, the women should be 'sedentary, still and stable' according to the manifest. The writers attack the modern-day feminists, who are said to exist because 'women are not presented with a true picture of man' which has resulted in them becoming confused. The message is that the only real men are members of ISIS.

'Women gain nothing from the idea of their equality with men apart from thorns.' Those 'thorns' are the fact they must work the same hours as men, despite their menstruation and pregnancies and 'responsibilities to their husband, sons and religion'. In the caliphate this has of course been organized much better. Because if a woman must really work there, in one of the few professions permitted for women, then they will not have long hours, there must be childcare available and she has a right to two months of maternity leave.

Women in the caliphate must reflect 'the women first called to religion', and then a list follows with not only 'our' Maria (who for Islam as the mother of the Prophet Jesus is also sacred), and the daughter of the Prophet Mohammed, Fatima, along with the 'women of the Companions [of the prophet, JN] and their followers' who are also 'the mothers of the believers'. And to rub it in even a bit more: woman 'was created from Adam and for Adam', and God has decided that 'there was no responsibility greater for her than that of being a wife to her husband'.

The manifest discusses in great detail 'the Divine duty of motherhood', but also the superiority of the man, whereby the woman has been given 'the honor of implementation'. She must do what she is told. The manifest is trying to portray this as an honorable command. Remarkably, it also concludes that the woman cannot fulfil her duty if she is 'illiterate or uneducated', and that Islam does not forbid education for girls, as long as it is not about 'useless' worldly sciences, but rather about knowledge about the Quran and Sharia. Education is allowed, but only to ensure that the women do not stray from the faith, and can pass along the knowledge to their children.

Girls can marry from the age of nine, as is also stated in the manifest. Between the ages of seven and fifteen they can be instructed in the study of Islam, Islamic history, the Sharia, and in skills such as sewing and cooking. How she would then ever be able to become a doctor or teacher, puzzles me.

They are exempted from the 'sedentary' lifestyle if they are a doctor or teacher. Those are the only two professions which are permitted for women, besides membership to the Khansa brigade. Next to that, women may study theology, and for this reason, they are even permitted to leave the house.

There is one more exception: if women are called up by a fatwa, they are permitted to fight in the jihad. Normally, that is not allowed for women, because fighting is a man's business. But apparently the leadership decided there could at some time be a situation which might arise, when all help is needed, also from the women. This is why all foreign women after their arrival and as part of their training, which mainly consists of an ideological education, receive also lessons in handling and firing a gun. But for the time being, only men can reach paradise via suicide attacks – despite similar organizations such as Al-Qaida and Boko Haram (in Nigeria) having recruited women to this end. With ISIS, the perpetrators will at the very most wear women's clothing, in an effort to avoid drawing attention to themselves when they carry out an attack.

If you are to believe the writers of the manifest, the situation in Mosul and Raqqa equals a paradise on earth. Clean and safe, women are not harassed, thanks to their concealing clothing and the tough action taken for every violation of the rules. It is proudly reported that women may travel from Mosul to Raqqa without having to show their faces even once at a checkpoint, in contrast to outside the caliphate where a woman with a niqaab cannot pass any checkpoint without identifying herself and showing her face.

≈ ≈ ≈

I try to imagine what the women are like, who composed this document. How much have the leaders of ISIS deleted; how much was rewritten? Do they actually believe what they have written? Such as: 'When the Islamic State fully undertook administration of the land, the people regained their rights, none more so than women'. But then I recall the role the followers, soldiers and security agents of Saddam Hussein played and still continue to play in the planning, framework and realization of the caliphate. During Saddam's rule, for reason of the emphasis on it, safety was better than it is in present day Iraq and Syria – even though this at the same time created a lack of freedom. With the current corruption and insecurity in those countries in the back of the mind, it is not illogical that the creators of the manifest praise the Islamic courts of the caliphate as a place where a woman can openly discuss any topic, without her having to negotiate or pay any bribes.

At the same time, it sounds good that the caliphate has a so-called Zakat-Room for the poor, as can be read in the manifest, where women can receive financial assistance; zakat is the obligation in the Islamic faith to give a portion of your income to the poor. The health care system is said to be better than ever, now that the sexes are separated in the hospitals.

However, from both Raqqa and Mosul reports are emerging about ever-increasing poverty amongst the civilians; a growing number of people are now reliant on soup kitchens. The caliphate is a society of great inequalities: while during the Ramadan pictures are circulated of fighters enjoying plentiful meals after breaking the fast, at the same time there are long lines of those waiting at the soup kitchens. The division of the sexes in the health care system works detrimentally for women, because for a large number of medical procedures there is a shortage of female physicians. A jihadi bride complained for example on Twitter about the incompetent care she received during childbirth, which resulted in the loss of her child. Other women report that during the delivery, where only women are permitted, they still had to wear a hijab.

In the manifest Raqqa is praised as being the place to be for immigrants, because 'lineages are mixed, tribes are merged and races join under the banner of monotheism'. And in making it really idyllic: Immigrant 'families in Raqqa live in peace and are untouched by hunger, the cold winds or frost'.

≈≈≈

The manifest confirms just how extremist the foreign women of ISIS really are. I know that converts are often stricter in their believes than the people who were born into the religion, and I noticed that this is especially true for women. The ISIS women are just as radical as the men.

Even though women are officially condemned to the kitchen, they do indeed have some influence at all levels of the caliphate. This is why I am so interested the report that the wives of high-ranking ISIS administrators play a role in the communication. As their husbands are being watched by the Americans and others, and their email and telephones can no longer be trusted, some of the most sensitive information is transmitted by their wives who recount the information through their network until it ends up at the right location.

How active women are, becomes clear from the story of Saja al-Dulaimi, who in 2009 for three months was married to Abu Bakr al-Baghdadi. It was an arranged marriage, intended to bind the influential Dulaimi tribe to Baghdadi's planned caliphate. She was his third wife and they have a daughter together, but details about their marriage are absent.

Dulaimi was in the news at the end of 2014, when she and her then five-year-old daughter were arrested in Lebanon, where she was raising funds for the radical Sunnis active in Arsal, on the border with

Syria. In many ways, she seems to be an exception in the strict Islamic culture. Both before and after her divorce to Baghdadi, she is said to have been married to other radical front men. She was also divorced from her first husband, and the second one perished in battle.

It is clear that this woman, who according to a Lebanese official involved in her arrest, is 'exceptionally beautiful', is highly devoted to radical Islam. You can consider her 'a child of Al-Qaida', which makes her the shining example for many female recruits from the West. All the more so, because during the interrogation following her arrest she reportedly did not reveal any useful information. Only through a DNA test could it be determined that her daughter is indeed a child of Baghdadi – whose genetic material is in the possession of the Americans because he spent five years in their Iraqi prisons.

When the Lebanese arrested her, Dulaimi was involved as a courier; she was smuggling gold and cash under her Islamic clothing to Lebanon. Various leaders of radical groups have brought their families to Arsal, in relative safety and still not too far from the battle. She reportedly was able to raise 200,000 dollars (€171,000), and delivered it to the movement in Arsal, making use of the custom of conservative societies where male guards may not search women.

Saja al-Dulaimi comes from a conservative Islamic and militant family; her father and brothers were killed in Iraq in the fight against the Americans. Her sister was arrested in the Kurdish capital Erbil in 2009, Govand Baban, a Kurdish lawyer friend told me: a sixteen-year-old who had strapped on an explosive belt to carry out an attack. He described her as being calm and nice. When I spoke to him at the beginning of 2016, she had already been incarcerated for seven years without having ever been convicted; and this former sister-in-law of Baghdadi would never be freed again, he said. 'In these kinds of situations human rights do not play a role. She is too close to Baghdadi. She can only leave her cell through a prisoner exchange.' He suggests she could be exchanged for Kurds whom ISIS has captured. Important pawns on this chessboard are held for just such an exchange, although this would never happen openly, as the Kurdish authorities in Erbil have officially declared that they do not in any way conduct business with ISIS.

≈≈≈

Women have been on various levels accomplices in the cruelty taking place in the caliphate. They help with the implementation, but are also involved in the leadership, as the example of Umm Sayyaf clearly shows. For that reason, I want to mention an investigation regarding the role of women during war and violence, in which Dutch criminologist Alette

Smeulders in 2015 concluded that women can be just as ruthless and cruel as the men – which is something the Yazidi women in Iraq and Syria know all too well.

Smeulders examined the role of women during the genocide in Rwanda – where they cheered on the murderers – the Nazi regime and different violent conflicts, concluding that women play a much bigger role in large-scale violence than previously known.

She found that most of the women are involved indirectly, for example by supporting a criminal regime and the criminal behavior of their husband. Many women also play an administrative or other supportive role in the organization of violence. A significant number of women are directly involved, for example through means of betrayal, theft and by guarding prisoners. Along with all of this, women also are involved in sexual violence against both men and women: not only by selecting victims or holding them captive, but also as a direct physical offender in a gang rape.

The complete details of the fate of the Yazidi women in the hands of ISIS women have by no means been made known, but for what we do know, Smeulders' description is accurate. She concludes, that women are in no way inferior to men in a context of both mass and collective violence. They are capable of assault, abuse, torture and murder. Although the criminologist has no explanation why women do this, she does determine that they are not 'psychologically disturbed monsters', as they are often portrayed to be, nor do they only act under force. That is an interesting assumption, even if 'do what society expects of you' is very close to force. 'It is time we accept the fact, that many female perpetrators are normal women, and that normal women just like normal men can become involved in large-scale violence,' according to Smeulders.

It is, after all, about the power and being able to deal with it. And this is something I have come across quite a bit in the Middle East. Often I had problems with guards and other lower officials who were unable to deal with the power their function encompassed, ruling like dictators over their own little empire. It is a reaction to the decade-long oppression in the region. They only know the abuse of power, and then copy what they know. Women are the worst, in my experience. This comes from the fact that they must survive in a male dominated society; they are afraid to make a mistake and overcompensate this with strictness. I am reminded of the female guards of government buildings, whom I always fight with because they not only prevent me from taking my phone inside, but also want to confiscate my flash drives. And of the female controllers who at airports test your perfume and confiscate your toothpicks.

You can see it all over the world: women adapt in

order to remain in control, and hide their insecurities by exhibiting and abusing power. In the caliphate, especially the Yazidi women are victim to this. But somehow I find women who turn on other women far worse, than when a man does it. Wasn't it Madeleine Albright, the former minister of Foreign Affairs of the United States who said that there was 'a special place in hell for women who do not help other women'?

≈≈≈

The Yazidi women in the caliphate are left to their own devices – and to their good luck of ending up with a kind Western fighter. From the stories of the Yazidi women, I discover that these treat them far better than the local fighters, as in the case of Khanu, the woman who lived with her two sons with the Afghan doctor and his three wives. Especially the wives made Khanu's life a living hell – with the exception of the one who became her friend and later helped her to escape.

But before her escape, Khanu twice ended up with a German. The first used the name Mohamed al-Almani (Mohamed the German) and was around fifty years old. During the ten days before he resold her, he locked her in a room, except when she had to do the housekeeping. Otherwise he treated her fairly; in any case without the usual beating.

There was an entire German community in the town where he lived; the fighters visited one another at home and also met outside the house. They spoke German with one another. As Mohamed did not speak a word of Arabic, it was no surprise that when he had to go to the frontline, he sold Khanu to someone from his German network. This Omar, who was in his thirties and had probably arrived in Germany as a migrant, had left his wife behind. He gave Khanu permission to move around freely inside the house.

That the non-Arabs treated the Yazidi women better, Hanna also discovered, who with two sisters and a fourth Yazidi woman had been sold to Russian ISIS fighters in Raqqa. 'We were taken to an army base which used to belong to Assad. There we went to a big house, where we were each given a room,' she said inside a tent in one of the refugee camps. Politely but sternly, she has sent away a curious boy, in order to be able to talk freely. I remember the attractive 25-year-old, who wore her hair in a ponytail and was dressed in a black t-shirt and a wine-red skirt, especially for the sad but wise look in her eyes.

She had been bought for 800 dollars (€684) by Alexander, a Christian who after converting to Islam called himself Abdullah. He had two other wives, one in Russia and one in Egypt, whom he had regular contact with by phone or Skype. He had already been in Syria for two years.

The house had four floors and was occupied by several ISIS fighters. Hanna: 'We lived on the second floor, my sister lived there too. Sometimes we were left alone for hours. Several fighters lived downstairs – they did not speak to us.' The women did not mind this; at least they were together during the day. 'We cooked for the men, and talked amongst ourselves. They talked mostly about the war and the air strikes. I heard from the Russian who had bought me, that he wanted to go to Kobani, which he said ISIS would conquer. I was sure that the Kurds would get the city back thanks to the air strikes.' And she was right, the Kurds managed to retake the Syrian city, although completely destroyed, after months of fierce fighting.

Hanna eventually was left alone with one sister, when the other two women were resold. The men, who talked with the sisters about Russia and even taught them a bit of Russian, said that they were happy with their lives in the caliphate. 'There was not a single negative word, they did what they were told.'

She said that she was aware of the fact that they were in reasonably good hands, as many Iraqi fighters would beat their women. And that she was far better off than her other sister, who ended up with an emir from Ukraine who already had two jihadi brides from Europe. This sister told her that she had even been given electric shocks; the Ukrainian was no better than the Iraqis.

≈≈≈

The continually reselling of the girls is not without risk, as became clear when an Indonesian fighter in June of 2015 was discovered to be infected with HIV, as peace activists in Syria reported. This was discovered when he had to donate blood for his wounded brothers-in-arms. Then it also became known, that the fifteen-year-old Yazidi girl in his possession was also infected, just like the Egyptian who had bought her from him.

But the contamination did not end there. He had the habit of loaning the girl out to his guests, and two Saudis also became infected in this way, just like an emir of ISIS. It is not clear if the chain ended there, but that is unlikely because there is also a good chance that they too have infected their 'slaves' and through them others still.

The Indonesian was aware of the fact he was infected when he arrived in Syria. ISIS executed him for 'spreading the deadly AIDS virus in the caliphate'.

≈≈≈

According to Hanna, mainly the Arabic fighters resold the women. 'Alexander was not planning to,' she said. 'Even though he sometimes joked about it. But when one of his friends warned him that all

Yazidi girls had to convert, he became so angry that he beat me and threatened to sell me.' Up until that time, unlike most of the other fighters, he had not forced her to pray and study the Quran, because he did not know that this was mandatory. Hanna was shocked by his threat. 'I begged him on my knees and kissed his feet to be allowed to stay with him – also because my sister was still with me. What else could I do?'

When Hanna described her daily life, I completely understood her behavior. In her region, many foreign ISIS fighters lived. 'We were allowed to go outside to do the shopping, as long as we wore a burqa. We could also go to an internet cafe this way, without being recognized.'

The freedom she had was unprecedented. And out in the streets she was even greeted. 'All foreign fighters had a wife and children, whom they had brought along. The women did the housekeeping, the shopping and brought the children to school.'

Alexander brought another wife from Russia. He had been successful in recruiting a jihadi bride as a third wife. Because they both had their own rooms, Hanna hardly saw her. The young Russian was divorced and had a two-year-old son. She bragged to Hanna that she would be going to the frontline. 'She had a gun and showed me a picture of her in military uniform.' I concluded that because she often left the house, she had probably joined the Khansa brigade, as well as playing a role in ISIS' recruitment. Since she spoke Russian, she was a valuable asset. Hanna heard her at work, without realizing what she was doing: 'I heard her talking with girls in sound fragments on WhatsApp'.

There were many reasons for hostilities between the two women, but Hanna does not mention any incidents. She herself became pregnant from Alexander, and he told this to his Russian bride. 'He was very happy. He wanted to increase the number of Muslims, he said. To have more jihadists.'

Whether the pregnancy was the reason for trying to escape, I do not know. I hear from aid workers that for many Yazidi women it was a reason to stay instead; many pregnant Yazidi women wanted to first give birth, because the shame of returning home pregnant was far too great to bear, and because they wanted to leave the child of their rapist behind.

Thanks to her relative freedom, Hanna managed to escape. She was able to get to an internet café with her sister, where they contacted a cousin. He planned the escape. They were picked up at an address by someone who was part of the network Yazidis had built in Syria to help the women escape. With false identification cards they were taken across the Turkish border, and from there on to Iraqi Kurdistan.

≈≈≈

When I spoke with Hanna, her stomach was flat and there were no signs of any pregnancy. In first years, this is true for most of the escaped women and girls who had become pregnant during their time in captivity with ISIS. In a normal situation, this would be strange as an abortion is virtually impossible, although a pregnancy out of wedlock in the conservative Iraq would be a scandal. For the Yazidis however, an exception was made, although this happened in secret, and no official confirmation is offered. Aid workers told me that Hanna too had undergone an abortion, but she never mentioned this with a single word.

Even a nine-year-old girl, who managed to escape from ISIS, arrived in Iraqi Kurdistan pregnant, after having been raped by at least ten different men. She was immediately taken abroad to receive medical treatment, because it was believed that she would not survive an abortion in Iraq.

How many Yazidi women became pregnant is unclear. For all details the outside world is dependent on those who manage to escape. And those are mostly seriously traumatized women, who are embarrassed to talk about their own experiences and those of the other Yazidi women whom they spent a shorter or longer time together with.

Towards and after the liberation of Mosul in 2017, a number of Yazidi women returned home with their children conceived by ISIS-men. Even though women are welcomed back, their children are not. They are considered to be of mixed blood, and therefor not accepted in the Yazidi community. The Yazidi leadership tried to solve the problem by placing the children in orphanages, but some women refused to part with their children and sometimes even decided to stay with their ISIS-men.

Poet of the caliphate

The rules in the caliphate are strict for women, but there are exceptions. This is evident from the notoriety Syrian poet Ahlam al-Nasr received, the 'poet of the Islamic State'. Her bundle of poems The blaze of truth is highly read on the internet by ISIS supporters. Her status increased further thanks to her marriage in October of 2014 in Raqqa to Abu Usama al-Gharib, a propagandist of the radical Islam – initially for Al-Qaida, now for ISIS – who was born in Austria and works closely together with the ISIS leadership.

ISIS' house poet comes from Damascus. She radicalized after the people's revolt against President Assad in 2011 and the brutal quelling of it, and she eventually ended up with ISIS in early 2014.

She has written poetry in praise of ISIS-leader Abu Bakr-al-Baghdadi, and in a thirty-page essay she defends the decision to have a captured Jordanian pilot burned alive. She describes the caliphate as an Islamic paradise, where the leaders are honorable and the followers abide by the rules of the faith. Of one of Al-Nasr's poems all sentences begin with the letters from the word daesh, where she uses the very name that is hated within ISIS to swear her allegiance to the organization.

In her poems she describes the military triumphs of ISIS as a new dawn for Iraq (this verse was translated from Arabic to English by The New Yorker):

Ask Mosul, city of Islam, about the
lions –
how their fierce struggle brought
liberation.
The land of glory has shed its humiliation
and defeat
and put on the raiment of splendor.

After travelling through the caliphate, Al-Nasr describes Raqqa as a place of daily wonders, a city where believers are reborn in the old, original faith. There are in the caliphate 'many things that we only know from our history books', she writes.

Poems are an important part of the Arabic language and culture, while the Quran is deemed by many to be the pinnacle of the art of Arabic. Therefore, poems are also part of the radical Islam – even Al-Qaida leader Osama bin Laden was known for his poetry. And that is why the Khansa brigade is named after a poet, who after her conversion became a follower of the Prophet Mohammed.

7
RECRUITING IN THE WEST

'Listen to me! I love you more than I've loved anyone. You should be here with me. I can't stand to think of you in that corrupt country. I'll protect you. I'll shelter you from the world's evils. If you come and live with me, you'll see what a paradise me and my men are building. You'll be amazed. Here, people care about each other. They respect each other. We're one big family, and we've already made a place for you – everyone is waiting for you! You should see how happy the women are here. They used to be like you – lost. One of my friends' wives has arranged a program for your arrival. After the shooting lessons, she'll take you to a beautiful store, the only one in the country which sells fine cloth. I'll pay for everything. You'll establish your own little world with your new friends. I'm so excited for you to be here. Mélodie, my wife! Hurry up, I can't wait.'

This is how ISIS fighter Abu Bilel al-Firanzi recruits the young convert Mélodie. Or so he thinks to have recruited her, because he does not know that behind Mélodie on Facebook, actually the 31-year-old French journalist Anne Erelle hides. She attempts to follow the activities of the jihadists while impersonating a girl named Mélodie, trying while working undercover to get into contact with them in a safe manner. Erelle, who works as a freelancer for a French magazine, writes in the book In the Skin of a Jihadist: Inside Islamic State's Recruitment Networks an account of the discussions she had as the twenty-year-old Mélodie with the jihadist who leads a unit of ISIS fighters in Syria and is involved in the recruiting process.

The 38-year-old Abu Bilel gets into contact with Mélodie, after she likes one of his You Tube videos. After they exchange some information and she tells him that she has converted to Islam without telling her mother, he does not waste any time. Via Skype, Facebook and text messages he aims straight for his target. 'You have converted, so... you should get ready for your hijrah,' he writes to Mélodie. While knowing virtually nothing about her yet, he asks the girl to 'immigrate' to a land at war.

More than 40,000 others from all over the world,

primarily men, but also women, have for the most part been recruited by ISIS over the internet in this way. They left their usually quiet life behind for what was promised to be a better life in the service of Allah.

'He was shamelessly inviting her to abandon her past, home and family [...] to be reborn in a new land,' Erelle writes. She concludes that Abu Bilel seeks out the weak, which have not enjoyed a stable youth or good education. Women, who are easy to convince.

Abu Bilel reveals himself to be a master in manipulation. 'He was like a salesman before making a pitch; he sought to understand the expectations and weaknesses of his prey,' Erelle writes. He speaks with Mélodie for example about the luxury of the West. 'While we're out risking our lives [so Muslims can live in their own state] you're spending your days with meaningless activities. [...] I'm worried about you, Mélodie, because I sense that you have a good soul, and if you continue to live among kafirs, you'll burn in hell'.

The message: if she does not come to Syria, she is a bad Muslim and will never get into heaven. Of course, a war is going on there and people are dying every day, 'I fight to stop that. [...] The enemy steals from and kills poor Syrians. He rapes women, too. He's attacking us, and we're defending peace'.

With this kind of dialogue, he tries to convince

young people from the West to join ISIS. And especially women, because the women are treated badly in the West, he claims. 'Men show you off like trophies.'

During their first talk via Skype, where Erelle is acting as Mélodie hiding behind a headscarf with a facial veil, he already asks her to marry him. 'You can trust me. You'll be really well taken care of here. You'll be important. And if you agree to marry me, I'll treat you like a queen'. Erelle later discovers that he already has three wives (from the ages of 20, 28 and 38) and three sons under the age of thirteen, of which the two eldest are already fighting on the frontlines. Mélodie would therefore be the fourth wife, but he does not tell her this.

Abu Bilel now has daily contact with 'his baby', as he has started calling Mélodie. He becomes ever more demanding, but also loose tongued. He proudly says that he is a cold-blooded killer, who for years has killed in the name of the faith. 'You are allowed to kill, as long as it's someone who doesn't respect Allah,' he tells Mélodie. 'You can burn them or strangle them, for example. Giving them a painful death is a service to Allah'.

At the same time, he tries to sell a life with ISIS as an adventure: 'Many women fantasize about us; we're Allah's warriors'. Married women have the right to go with their men to the frontline, he says. 'Sometimes we let our wives shoot – they love it!'

He serves up a life for her in which she can have fun with her friends while he is at the frontline. In the morning, she can have Arabic lessons, in the afternoon, she can visit hospitals or orphanages. He says that there are many French and Belgian women, and calls the female European recruits 'crazy' because they all want to have a Kalashnikov to use. While he promises her freedom, he emphasizes the fact that she must bring along a sitar because she needs this to be covered from top to toe.

Abu Bilel tells Mélodie that the jihadists have a preference for the female converts from the West. 'You're more serious about religion, and at the same time more open about life'. And when she asks what he means, it turns out to be about sex. The bottom line is that foreign women are more creative in bed, something Mélodie does not comment on with the primness expected of her. But Abu Bilel is unstoppable. 'You can do what you want with your husband when you are alone. [...] You need to fulfil his every wish. You can wear whatever you want underneath your sitar and burqa. Garter belts, fishnet stockings, anything your husband might like'. Does she like nice lingerie, he asks, then declaring that she is 'his'.

The jihadist pulls the net even tighter. As Erelle decides after ample consideration to allow Mélodie to agree to a marriage, she receives friend requests on Facebook from women both inside and outside the caliphate, in French, German and Arabic. Various women are considering travelling to Syria and want advice about what they should take along. Apparently he announced the marriage right away on Facebook.

Shortly after Abu Bilel orders Mélodie to choose a new Islamic name, he tells her that the marriage decree has been signed and that she is now officially his wife. The emir of Raqqa has already found a beautiful apartment for them. The pressure increases: 'Don't disappoint me. I've already told everybody you're coming, including the other brothers and the border police. [...] Be strong; come to Syria. You're a real lioness, my wife'.

When the appointment is made that she will travel together with a fifteen-year-old niece – which Erelle has had to make up, because Mélodie cannot travel alone – via Amsterdam and Istanbul to Syria, Mélodie is told to 'leave everything behind, cut all ties'. She is not even allowed to leave a goodbye letter for her mother: 'Just disappear, you can send news once you're here – and only then'. He tells her what kind of travel bag she must use, not to draw attention to herself, buy new telephones and to be careful with the police. In Turkey, there will be 'a mother' waiting for her who will help her on.

Hours later, Erelle sends a message via Skype that she and her niece were questioned at the Amsterdam airport and are being watched, which is why they have returned to France. He reacts furiously: 'Where are you, you little bitch? I swear to Allah, you're going to pay!' And then he threatens her: his friends have fifteen years of experience in counter espionage, he writes. 'We'll find you in a matter of minutes.'

Erelle discovers that Abu Bilel's first name is Rachid, that he was born in Roubaix as the son of French-Algerian parents and after quitting school ended up in crime. He radicalized, and visited a Quran school in Pakistan. In Iraq, he joined the resistance against the Americans, where he met Baghdadi, and he fought in Afghanistan and Libya. When he joined ISIS, he also brought his cousins to Syria. They all have the nickname al-Firanzi (the Frenchman), and they form a powerful clan within ISIS. He says that he gives orders to the 'French battalions': who goes to the frontlines, who must patrol in the cities and who must settle up with 'infidels whose time has come'. He also says that he organizes language classes for the recruits who do not speak Arabic. Abu Bilal turns out to be a big fish: he works closely with Abu Bakr al-Baghdadi himself.

≈≈≈

That is why Anna Erelle is an alias. The French police, who had without her knowledge been listening in on all of her communications, because they thought she was headed for Syria, arrested a number of people with whom Abu Bilel had brought her into contact. She discovers that a fatwa has been declared against her by ISIS, which calls for her to die a painful death.

Erelle moves house several times, changes her phone number often and even her identity. Where she was after publication of the book and what she was doing remained unknown, that's how seriously she and the police were taking the threats by ISIS. The story that she so very much wanted to publicize was in hindsight so dangerous, that she no longer could gain notoriety from it under her own name.

≈≈≈

The attempt to recruit Mélodie will likely not differ greatly from those for other foreign women and girls, some barely older than thirteen. How many women went to Syria from Europe, America, Australia and the Arab world is unknown. Estimates start at 4,000. What these women all likely have in common, is that there is something missing from their life, which leaves them at the mercy of the recruiters. Those offer lonely women friendship and purpose in their lives.

This for example is true regarding the 23-year-old American Christian Alex, who has converted to Islam and is considering a trip to Syria, all due to the influence of a recruiter named Faisal, who operates out of England. The conversations with him fill her empty days, the gifts he sends – books about Islam, Islamic clothing and chocolate – give her the feeling that she is appreciated, just like the many conversations via social media with a number of other ISIS supporters.

Alex, whose story was written down by The New York Times, leads a double life as she hides her conversion from her direct surroundings. When her grandmother, whom she lives with, finally discovers it, she is already so devoted to Faisal's attention that she secretly continues to stay in contact with him, despite having promised her grandmother that she would break it off. But she also puts into words the double feelings she has about the contact: 'I felt like I was betraying God and Christianity. But I also felt excited because I had made a lot of new friends.'

Her 'new friends' use Bible verses to convince her that Christ was indeed a prophet, but that the Prophet Muhammed came after him. And that in fact Islam is an improvement of Christianity. They follow the instructions from the book A course in the art of recruiting, which is compiled by ISIS' predecessor Al-Qaida in Iraq. This give the advise to spend as much time as possible with a possible recruit. The recruiter must 'listen to his conversation carefully' and 'share his joys and sadness' to get closer, which reminds me of the tactics used by 'lover boys' who seduce girls to work for them as prostitutes.

Following this, the recruiter must offer some basic

knowledge about Islam, but not yet talk about the jihad, the holy war. 'Start with the religious rituals and concentrate on them'. That is why Faisal sent the books about Islam to Alex.

The same methods are used by sects. You tie someone to you, making sure he becomes addicted to the contact, and then start to pry him loose from his trusted environment. There is a better life waiting, such a recruit is told, your real family is here with us. Do not listen to the lies being told about us. It all sounds so simplistic, but it works. Nasser Weddady, a Mauritanian American affiliated with the American Islamic Congress who investigates the way in which this form of recruiting can be combated best, says that 'all of us have a natural firewall in our brain that keeps us from bad ideas'. And that recruiters search for 'the weaknesses in the wall, and then attack'.

≈≈≈

The recruiters of ISIS are mostly men. That is true for those who recruited Mélodie, Alex and many other women, as long as they did not followed a family member or friend who had previously left for Syria. But since the summer of 2014, most of the women have come to Syria thanks to the recruitment practices of other foreign women.

Those women were given that task, because they were used to an active life in the West, while in the caliphate there is little else to do besides looking after their husband, getting pregnant and having children. They had to be kept busy to prevent any discontent. Moreover, they could utilize their own women's network in the West. Furthermore, it did not pertain to just a couple of cases, and because so many women were coming to Syria who unlike the men were not dying on the frontlines, an organization could be established for them, in which they could relay their knowledge and skills. Like Abu Bilel says in Erelle's book, foreign women are more serious, and they come to help to develop the Islamic state. They are more dedicated than the local Syrian and Iraqi women.

This is another reason why the Khansa brigade was established. An Uzbek woman, Dina Uzbek, is said to have led the recruiting effort by a large number of foreign women of the brigade in the Iraqi city of Mosul. They made contact with young people who via Twitter, Facebook or You Tube show interest in the activities of ISIS, just like Abu Bilel contacted Mélodie via Facebook after she liked one of his videos. Alex became prey after she asked for an explanation about the execution of American journalist James Fowley via social media.

Without question, the most famous foreign recruiter is Aqsa Mahmood, who is from Glasgow, and as a nineteen-year-old medical student left home in November of 2013 to join ISIS. As Umm

Layth (mother of the lion), she was very active on the internet; for a long time after her arrival in Syria she kept a blog on Tumblr.

Although she denied it, Mahmood is said to have brought the three British teenagers to Syria, who in the beginning of 2015 gained global notoriety when photos from numerous security cameras recorded their trip to the caliphate. The fifteen-year-olds Shamima Begum and Amira Abase and their sixteen-year-old girlfriend Kadiza Sultana were recruited in a matter of months, after Shamima was said to have been in contact with Mahmood via Twitter.

I want to reveal how the process of radicalization developed for Aqsa Mahmood, because if she could be lured to come to Syria, then that could happen to just about everyone.

She grows up in a liberal and prosperous Muslim family with four children. Her father was the first Pakistani cricketer to come to Scotland in the seventies. Mahmood attends a private school for girls, listens to Coldplay and loves Harry Potter books. She is not very religious and certainly has no radical ideas. And she cannot stand people shouting at one another.

'She was the best daughter you could ever wish for,' her saddened father says to CNN after her departure. 'She loved school. She was very friendly. In my entire life I have never raised my voice to her.'

The war in Syria leads to a change in his daughter.

She openly voices her concern about the violence, and begins to pray, reads the Quran and starts wearing a headscarf. That must have been the moment when she was recruited.

As became evident from Abu Bidel's words to Mélodie, ISIS is clearly using the war in Syria to create an 'us and them' atmosphere which is an important recruiting tool. Mahmood wants to become a doctor or pharmacist, but just barely passes her high school exams – which is common for young people in the recruitment process. She does continue her studies, but ceases listening to music and reading fiction. Her parents are not worried though, because she still goes to the movies and out to eat with her sisters.

In November of 2013, Aqsa Mahmood leaves her family home without saying a word to her parents, and travels to Syria – just like Abu Bilel had ordered Mélodie to do. In Syria she marries an ISIS fighter who is killed within a year, and so she is left as a widow.

On her blog on Tumblr one can read how hard she found it to leave her family. 'The first phone call you make once you cross the borders is one of the most difficult things you will ever have to do,' she writes. 'It is so difficult when you hear them sob and beg like crazy on the phone for you to come back. I can never do justice to how cold hearted you feel.' Yet she adds: 'But as long as you are firm and you know that this is all for the sake of Allah, then nothing can shake you, insha Allaah.'

Elsewhere she writes just as easily, that 'the family you receive in exchange for the one you left behind, is a pearl compared to the shell which you threw away in the sea'. Her blog unintentionally gives an impression of the indoctrination process. For instance when she writes that a parent with 'little Islamic knowledge and understanding' could never possibly grasp the idea of why a child would leave behind a life of luxury for the war, and therefore will continue to hope in vain that it will return back home. This is how ISIS splits the world into 'us and them'; parents are portrayed as being ignorant, in other cases as infidels, while ISIS claims to spread knowledge and the true faith.

To help instill the feeling of having a new family, or brother- or sisterhood, ISIS supporters consequently call one another 'brother' and 'sister'. Foreign couples call one another lion and lioness. Also the ISIS-speak, in which English (and German and French) is larded with Arabic words, must give the supporters the feeling that they belong.

I see this 'us and them', in another context, when Aqsa Mahmood as Umm Layth warns American and British leaders that 'we will overrun you and your countries and [...] destroy them' and that 'your blood will be spilled by our cubs'. Here she simply mimics the words of ISIS leaders, for example by using the word 'cubs', the little lions that are the future of the caliphate. Her nickname is her testimony that her goal is to be the mother of such a little lion.

Aqsa Mahmood pushes 'brothers and sisters who keep hanging on in the West' to 'hurry, hurry and hurry to our countries' in order to defend the Islamic faith. Because 'this is a war against Islam' and 'you are either with them or with us. Pick a side.' Elsewhere, she encourages young people to fight for ISIS because it is well rewarded with 'gifts from Allah', including 'a house with free electricity and water, thanks to the caliph who offers them without rent' and 'the even greater reward' in the life after death.

≈≈≈

Mahmood also gives advice to women who want to join ISIS. The future jihadi brides are told that they especially need to bring along a good pair of boots for the cold winters, and also makeup and jewelry. Because for your husband you will want to make yourself beautiful, she seems to indicate.

Sometimes, Mahmood briefly reveals on her blog as Umm Layth that the new life is also a bit disappointing for her. She clearly is in need of someone she can confide in. Not only does she miss her mother's smile and her shoulder as a resting place for her head: 'While most of you can still go and have that heart to heart talk with your mother, I cannot anymore.' It even sounds like a disguised warning, when in May of 2014 she writes: '...to recognize the worth and value of your mother, because once you lose her, nothing will be the same again.'

I can only conclude that the caliphate is not what she expected; that the friendships there are a disappointment to her, that she misses intimacy and compassion. This is also clear, when following the death of her husband, she complains that the caliphate has too little attention for the consequences of widowhood. That elegy however is swiftly censured away by other ISIS supporters, and her hash tag #nobodycaresaboutthewidow does not last long.

Somewhere on her blog, she reports the possibility to recruit parents through their children – as is common practice in cults. She writes, that she knows of parents who were angry with their daughters when they joined ISIS, but now 'are planning for a visit' with their daughters to 'this beautiful country'. Some do indeed come to the caliphate because a family member is already living there, although it is more often brothers or sisters instead of parents.

In June of 2015, three sisters with a British-Pakistani background leave for the pilgrimage to Mecca. There, Sugra (30), Khadija (33) and Zohra Dawood (34) take a flight to Istanbul with their total of nine children, to join their brother in the caliphate.

Their three husbands are left in the dark, and beg the sisters to return when they find out. 'We had a perfect relationship, a wonderful family,' says one of the two men to the British press. Some media report however that the arranged marriages were not that happy, and one of the marriages already ended in divorce, while another sister was living separated from her husband. Such a situation of course makes it much easier to leave.

≈ ≈ ≈

Recruiting not only takes place through the internet or by family, but also by radical imams in mosques. That happens in Iraqi Kurdistan for example, where an estimated 250 youths made contact with ISIS via Salafist imams. Also, from a number of jihadists who travelled from Cardiff to Syria, it is generally believed that they were recruited by an underground network of ISIS supporters, operating in their city.

The British political scientist Anthony Glees, who is affiliated with the University of Buckingham and who has authored six books about national security, told the British newspaper the Daily Mail that the recruiters in Wales look for victims at schools, on campuses and in Islamic centres. According to Glees, youths can become a target if they are idealists, interested in politics, angry about the situation in Palestine or the war in Iraq, and disappointed in the world around them. Glees says the recruiters know that if they manage to recruit a young person, he or she will not be able to break from the organization. 'I don't believe there are significant numbers of people going out to fight with the Islamic State, who get there and say, "Oh, this is terrible, and we were so wrong about believing in this".'

He concludes that there is nothing, society can do once the young people are there. 'They can certainly never be allowed to come back, because once they are radicalized, there is no way of bringing them back to British democratic values,' according to Glees, who points out their safety risk. 'They fight for a totalitarian system and against democratic values.'

That return and reintegration do not work, can be blamed on the professionalism of the recruiting. Journalist Anne Erelle speaks of 'Jihadists 2.0's new communication strategy': the combination of using the internet, the promises made to young people and the manner in which their emotions are tampered with. Erelle: 'Future jihadists are no longer attracted by the concept of earning easy money, guns or dealing in drugs. Instead, they dream of respect and acknowledgement. They want to be "heroes".'

≈≈≈

Participating in the building of an Islamic state, gaining a status, becoming part of a brother- or sisterhood, having a clear goal in life by fighting for something or giving birth to the next generation – these are all reasons to leave for the caliphate. But let's not forget about the powerful attraction of adventure. This generation, which spends many hours every day behind the computer, often playing violent computer games, encounters relatively little excitement in their daily lives.

Making the journey to the caliphate is in itself an adventure. Numerous teen-aged girls had previously barely travelled, when they answered the call of ISIS. For that reason, internet offers a number of instructions on how to organize a trip to Dawlah – the nickname all supporters lovingly use for al-Dawla al Islamiya (the Islamic state). Reading them, I am reminded of how youth trips are advertised.

For years, the trip went to the Turkish city of Istanbul, and from there by taxi or domestic flight to the border with Syria. ISIS does not pay for the tickets. Abu Bilel dryly advises his prey to steal the money for the trip from her parents. The trip is not so expensive, because for Turkey there are often cheap tickets available and domestic flights in Turkey are not expensive. But a young person still has to manage to gather a few hundred dollars.

Instructions for the journey come from amongst others Umm Waqqas, of whom the media originally reported that she was either British or Dutch and operated from Raqqa. She co-authored an online instruction book for young people, Hijrah to the Islamic State. This brought her into contact with several foreigners who wanted to travel to Syria, including a number of Americans, who were arrested by the FBI, and two girls from Colorado who were stopped during a layover in Germany. She also exchanged messages with Umm Layth (Aqsa Mahmood).

On her Twitter account, with 8,000 followers, Umm Waqqas supported ISIS and defended their atrocities, such as the burning alive of a Jordanian pilot. According to the instruction book, she is a contact person who can help you join ISIS. In a tweet, she warns those who are interested in joining, not to share that information with anyone: 'The sharing of your intention to make hijrah can: 1. corrupt your intentions; 2. ensure that you will be arrested. Remember: trusting everyone is stupid.'

In April of 2015, the British Channel 4 revealed the identity of Umm Waqqas: it turned out to be Rawdah Abdisalaam, an American of Somalian descent living in the American city of Seattle, who gave up studying journalism to become a teacher. Her own process of radicalization could be followed on Twitter, where she posted more and more radical tweets, instead of the earlier tweets about American football, pizzas and hamburgers. Although she denied everything to Channel 4, she appears to be a recruiter who operates from her residence. After her Twitter account had been discontinued, she disappeared once again from view.

A single journalist suggests that she was a 'honey pot': that she attracted young people who were radicalizing and because of this could be discovered and stopped, which is indeed what happened to a number of them. It is not even such a strange thought, that the secret services would use a decoy in order to thwart the efforts of the recruiters. How else could you discover potential recruits in time?

What does this mean for the instruction book in which she is named? That appears to be authentic, not so much for the advices given, but rather regarding the many details. An American recruiter for ISIS, who is only known under the Twitter name @Abdul_Aliy_4, not only advises people what to bring along (what fits into a travel bag and a backpack, but don't forget your flashlight and your nail clippers), but in a special chapter for 'sisters' he even attempts to 'virtually' lead women through Turkey.

Beforehand, they must make contact with the border office of ISIS, the Madrasat al-Hudūd, and are told to save its telephone numbers under another name (not as Osama bin-Laden, he emphasizes, half-jokingly). They are instructed to obtain a new Turkish SIM card after arriving in Turkey (and only one from Turkcell, with a range reaching across the border into Syria). The border office will instruct them what to do, usually to take a flight to the Turkish place Sanliurfa, also known as Urfa, where ISIS has a strong presence.

≈ ≈ ≈

Until June of 2015, that was the main route for travelling to the caliphate: from Urfa to the Syrian Tal Abyad, and from there to Raqqa. That last stretch is only 80 kilometers long. After the Kurds conquered Tal Abyad, ISIS lost this connection between Turkey and Syria. New routes had to be found. It became even more difficult to get across the border after the Turks in August of 2015 joined the American coalition against ISIS. They then closed a number of border offices, and picked up groups of people at the border heading to Syria. And when the predominantly Kurdish SDF, which was supported by the Americans, in Syria in 2016 and 2017 conquered more and terrain from ISIS, entering the country and thus what was by then left of the caliphate became ever more difficult.

In the instruction book, the American recruiter insists that the women do not travel in groups, but in pairs, and on a tourist visa, thus drawing as little attention to themselves as possible. They are to follow the orders they receive at the border office, patiently wait for their ISIS contact persons and not panic, even if they are late – they will really come, he reassures them. They will then be taken to the house of an ISIS supporter, so that later on they can cross the border in the dark. That house has a room especially for women, with a door that can be locked, and there will be food and drinks, the American writes. He emphasizes that they must put an extra abaya, a long, wide dress in their backpack and wear 'the most comfortable sneakers ever'. Because they will have to run for a distance at the border, and crawl under barbed wire which might tear their clothes.

It sounds like an adventure, and I believe that is how it was intended. From the travel stories of young people who went to Syria in this internet book, I can conclude that for many youths this was the attraction. A 'sister' recounts how she was stopped by Turkish border police and almost sent back home. She and her girlfriend ended up in jail, but managed to phone ISIS who sent a lawyer and miraculously had them released in no time, and then helped them get across the border.

Once they are across the Syrian border, the women went to the headquarters of the Khansa-brigade in Raqqa. Married women who had come to join their husbands quickly exchanged this for a single-family home, but single women remained there until a marital partner was found, or they were temporarily housed under the supervision of an older woman in a nearby home.

ISIS had a special office which focuses on bringing

together fighters and brides. Both were to submit a request if they want to marry.

But women did not join ISIS primarily to marry a fighter, according to researchers of the Institute for Strategic Dialogue (ISD) and the International Centre for the Study of Radicalization (ICSR) from London's King College. For the investigation Till Martyrdom Do Us Part: Gender and the ISIS Phenomenon they looked at roughly a hundred women in Syria and Iraq, and their comments on Twitter, Facebook and Tumblr. Those women were from fifteen countries and spoke mainly English amongst themselves.

The researchers listed as important reasons why young women were joining ISIS, the purported oppression of Muslims in the West and the power of attraction from the idea of sisterhood. For many women, marriage to a fighter was not the main issue. They felt like 'pilgrims with a mission to develop an Islamic utopia in the region,' the researchers concluded.

Moreover, they too wanted to go to the frontline. Just how eager they were, I can conclude from the photos posted by a number of foreign ISIS women on social media, in which they are posing with Kalashnikovs and in one instance in front of a BMW owned by a spouse. I try to understand the contrast: hidden away under a burqa, posing in front of a fast car. Is it about the eroticism, the status or about a great and exciting adventure? That weapon and the car as a counterweight for the invisibility?

It is also significant to know how eager the foreign women were to hit the streets with the armed Khansa brigade. They were given lessons in firing a weapon - in case that some time, they would be allowed to fight for the caliphate. But did that weapon possibly give them a sense of power?

Power and powerlessness definitely played a role. In their recruitment rhetoric, the ISIS women simply reduced the world's conflicts to the difference between good and evil. The British researchers saw this as an alluring topic for people who are disappointed in the world and have turned away from it, because by travelling to the caliphate they see an opportunity to be a 'hero', to do good, to save the world.

Young women are sensitive to this type of rhetoric because they are often in doubt about their own identity. According to the British research, many women have revealed that they felt socially or culturally isolated in the secular Western society. They saw the region under ISIS's control as 'a safe enclave for those who wish to embrace and protect the Islamic faith'.

On social media, the women were continually talking about the camaraderie they have found in the caliphate, and they posted pictures of themselves posing with their black-clothed 'sisters'. Thus, they created a contradiction with their earlier false feelings and superficial friends in the West, the researchers concluded. 'For many women, the search for meaning, sisterhood, and identity is the main driving force'.

But girls will be girls, and therefore they also long for romance, for being 'one', being together with a husband. 'On the internet, images of a lion and lioness are used as the symbol for this unity,' according to the research. 'This is symbolic for finding a brave and strong husband, but it also propagates the notion that women by marrying a jihadist and embracing the ISIS ideology, become stronger themselves.' Most of the women did realize that marrying a jihadist meant not having a long life together. This is evident from the story of jihadi bride Sham, a doctor who worked for ISIS, and found her husband via an arranged meeting. She posted a picture from her wedding on social media: he with a beard and tie, she in a white burqa, with the black flag of ISIS in the background. Beneath that romantic picture she wrote: 'Marriage in the land of the jihad: until the martyrdom do us part'.

Recruiters used stories about women who dine together by candlelight and bathe in the Euphrates, but most of the young migrants quickly discovered that the reality in the caliphate was far more stark. And yet little criticism did get out, as a quibbler would immediately be set upon by the rest of the ISIS recruiting network. On the other hand, ISIS women warned new recruits that they would be 'put to the test' through power outages, water shortages, cold winters and living in a war zone. And the censorship was not complete: one Western woman reported having a miscarriage, because she could not communicate with the doctor at the ISIS hospital.

≈≈≈

For some women, the disappointment over what they found with ISIS was such, that they chose not to stay. For example, the Dutch girl Aicha from Maastricht. She is called Sterlina, until she converts to Islam, takes on the name of Aicha and radicalizes. In February of 2014, she travels to Syria to marry the Turkish-Dutch jihadist and former soldier Omar Yilmaz. That marriage is dissolved after a few months, and Aicha sends her mother a desperate call for help, saying that she wants to leave, but cannot get out of Raqqa.

In November, her mother Monique is successful in getting her out of the caliphate. I am curious about how she managed to do this, but she refused to reveal any details. According to some media she travelled to Raqqa in a burqa, but the Dutch Public Prosecutor said she was never actually in Syria. That is why I suspect that Aicha and her mother had help from within the caliphate, and kept silent about this to protect those people.

Aicha did claim to British media that Yilmaz 'used me as a slave and threw me away.' But Yilmaz denied this. 'She had a good life as a housewife,' he said and added: 'we parted ways as friends because it did not work'. Aicha claimed however, that he had given her away to a Tunisian jihadist. In any case, she could not remain with ISIS alone, so a marriage would have been arranged for her after Yilmaz left. On her return to the Netherlands, Aicha was arrested and accused of cooperating with a terrorist organization, but was released a few days later on probation and with strict conditions. I hope that one of those conditions was participating in a de-radicalization program to undo the indoctrination of ISIS. The de-radicalization of people returning from Syria is a global problem the world is going to have to deal with.

How can someone like this function again in the Dutch society? In March of 2015, the Dutch newspaper De Telegraaf reported that Aicha had escaped from a justice department safe house and once again had married a Salafist, and continuously wore her burqa when she went out, even in the Netherlands. In the words of British Professor Glees: 'They are lost. Once they have become extremists, they are that forever.'

≈ ≈ ≈

The fate of another young Dutch woman, Laura

Hansen, only becomes known when she arrives in July 2016 at a Kurdish frontline with her husband and two children, after having lived in the caliphate for ten months. The same evening of her flight, she states to the Kurdish TV station K24 that her life was 'a hell' there. The general at the frontline tells me a few days later, that ISIS fired at them, and Laura left her wounded husband behind, stating that he was 'a bad ISIS and a bad man'. After two weeks of interrogations, the Kurds turn Laura over to the justice department in the Netherlands.

As often with jihadists, Laura's story is filled with gaps. She is seventeen, when she converts to Islam and marries Dutch Palestinian Ibrahim Ismael through an Islamic dating site. Together they live according to the rules of the Salafist Islam, and leave in September 2015 to Syria, only days after their youngest son has been circumcised. Laura later tells K24 about domestic violence, but from sources near to them, I get the impression of a close couple that decides together to travel to Syria. Laura's statements that she was taken by her husband without her knowledge to ISIS territory, are not supported.

Unlike many other jihadists, the couple never breaks the ties with their families at home. As they have regular contact with both, it is known that they are not happy at all in the caliphate and are considering escape. But the way they eventually do so, surprises all: they arrive suddenly in the morning at the frontline, after not having mentioned any such plans during a late night contact with the home front. Trying to cross an active frontline in broad daylight is very dangerous, and their escape seems to stem mainly from panic.

A source at the Kurdish secret service vows to me that Laura has worked for the Kurds, by phoning them in secret with information about the location of important ISIS fighters. If that is true, Laura can hardly have done that on her own; women are not even allowed to go out alone. Was her husband involved, and were they found out by ISIS, therefore having to leave in a hurry?

It seems Laura had no choice but to leave her husband during the flight, as he was shot in both the leg and his abdomen. If ISIS considers him a spy, that can lead to an execution – is that the reason why the Kurds decide to tell the story that Laura left him as 'a dirty ISIS' behind? Whatever is the case, a year later the Iraqi army manages to arrest the husband who is then part of an attack near to the Syrian border. He is later sentenced to death in Baghdad.

≈ ≈ ≈

Only six months before Laura's escape, Kurdish commandos saved a young Swedish woman from the caliphate; because her parents went and begged the Peshmerga to do so, it was said. Laura's father is also said to have asked them for help. But does such a demand really lead to action, or was the Swedish girl also actively collecting information for the Kurds?

While ISIS is getting weaker from 2016, and losing more and more terrain, many disenchanted recruits try to leave the sinking ship. If ISIS catches them escaping, they are executed for treason. At the same time, the group has started to actively send back foreign supporters to Europe to plan and carry out attacks.

Whatever role Laura was playing, the justice system in the Netherlands has had to check her story carefully. Because it was considered possible that the stories of disenchantment were a smoke screen, and the couple was on the road to Europe on orders from ISIS.

Laura was eventually freed by the end of 2017, after having served a jail sentence. Her children were given in care to her parents, and Laura went back to study wearing an ankle bracelet to monitor her movements.

A special family

Migrants stick together in the caliphate, and just like it is true for the Brits, Russians and Germans, it is for

Australian jihadists, as the story of two Australian friends, Khaled Sharrouf and Mohammed Elomar, illustrates. Because Sharrouf is married to an Australian woman who has converted to Islam, the Australian media closely follow their adventures.

Sharrouf's wife Tara Nettleton and their five children have joined him in Syria, but the wife of Elomar is stopped at the airport on the way out, along with their three children. Soon after their arrival, Sharrouf's wife and eldest daughter Zaynab become active on social media. They post pictures of the youngest children, posing with weapons. When Sharrouf, who now calls himself Abu Zarqawi al-Australi (the Australian), posts a photo of his little boy holding up the head of a Syrian soldier, the Australian media almost explode with disgust. The caption of the picture is taunting: 'That's my boy!'

To solve the problem that Elomar, who now calls himself Abu Hafs al-Australi now is without a wife, the fourteen-year-old Zaynab marries him. She then calls herself Umm Hafs and her Twitter account shows her accepted into the circle of women and widows of Australian fighters. They pose together, armed and completely dressed in black, in front of a white BMW. 'Chillin in the khilafah, lovin life,' she writes.

The Sharroufs also have Yazidi slaves, as is clear when one of them manages to escape. A nineteen-year-old woman tells the Australian site News.com.au that she was being held with six other girls in their house just outside of Raqqa. Sharrouf had chosen her and another girl as his nikah (concubine); the others had to do the housekeeping. She was able to escape when Sharrouf was at the frontline.

8

LIFE UNDER OCCUPATION

At the height of ISIS' rule, an estimated five to eight million people are living in the caliphate, an area straddling Syria and Iraq which equals the size of Switzerland (41,285 square kilometers). The society can be roughly split into those who belong to ISIS, and those who are living under occupation. Citizens who are in danger have fled, because they are Christians or Shiites, or belong to the Yazidi or Shabak minorities. So have citizens, politicians and civil servants who had ties to the Shiite government in Baghdad, and those who knew that they did not want to live under the Sharia law.

But thousands did remain in what is now an entirely Sunni society. They stayed, because they had no money, because they did not want to leave their house and possessions behind or because they thought that the ISIS regime would not last for very long, and that they could tolerate it as long as they went unnoticed.

Some men who saw the looming storm clouds, eventually sent their families out of the city, but in Raqqa, Mosul and other places where ISIS had seized control, most of the women remained. Many were used to a great deal: violence in the streets, kidnappings, bombings. How much worse could it get?

Initially, safety improved under ISIS. Demonic measures, such as chopping off the hands of thieves, resulted in much less being stolen. The corruption disappeared, and one no longer had to buy services. Streets were cleaner. The only remaining violence came from ISIS, so at least that was clear.

In the summer of 2015, thousands of Sunni refugees fled to the Iraqi ISIS bastion Mosul. They were fleeing the battle in the Anbar province, and had nowhere else to go. That had resulted in images of desperate women who walked with their children through the heat, in search of a safe place. The Shiite government in Bagdad did not want to grant them entry, because they might have ties to ISIS, and also in the Kurdish region many were refused due to security concerns.

The Syrian ISIS capital city of Raqqa also received

refugees from cities where the battle between ISIS and Syrian Kurds, but also with other resistance groups, was running high. While it was known that ISIS had transformed Raqqa from a fairly progressive provincial city into one, where compliance of the Sharia laws was enforced with a heavy hand, no one was prepared for what this would in fact mean.

≈≈≈

After the fall of Mosul in June of 2014, I have maintained contact with acquaintances from the city, who for the most part fled to Kurdistan. One of my best friends originates from Mosul. His father has stayed behind, with a son who cares for him. From time to time, I call a journalist there who also fled to the safety of Erbil. And because I know the ousted governor Nujaifi and his son Abdullah, I can question them about the situation.

And that is worsening. On the first anniversary of the takeover, the first thing my contact person mentions is the position of the women, as the dress rules have only just been changed for a third time. After the niqaab, followed the veil which covers the entire face, the sitar. And then billboards announce that only a burqa in combination with gloves is still acceptable.

It is not only the most visible change, but is a symbol for what has happened to Mosul – and probably elsewhere in the caliphate. This already fairly conservative city has under ISIS developed into a kind of Afghanistan – it is no coincidence most of the ISIS fighters walk around wearing long Afghan shirts and wide pants. Following the example of the feared Taliban in Afghanistan – where many fighters have fought – all personal freedoms have been restricted.

For the men of the city, this also has consequences. The 29-year-old Ali, who now lives in Erbil, has a cousin and peer in Mosul with whom he is in regular contact. Until the young man has a full beard and long hair, he cannot go out, Ali tells me in May of 2015, shaking his head in disbelief. Only men older than 45 are permitted to trim their beards. Shaving is forbidden. There is a fine for this of 100,000 dinar (€72/$85) and a prison sentence of a week. For a second conviction, the punishment is forty lashes and thirty days imprisonment.

A few months later, I am told this is part of the defensive plan of ISIS for the city, just like the digging of ditches around the city's border. Rumors about an attempted recapturing of the city are mounting; a number of times the Americans even drop flyers in which they call upon the civilians to help the 'liberation army' when it reaches the city. By forcing all of the men to look just like the ISIS supporters, the enemy will no longer be able to differentiate between them.

Smoking has become even more prohibited than it already was. If it can be smelled on someone's fingers that he smokes, he will be punished by breaking his fingers. A second conviction means they will be chopped off.

At the same time, the ban on smoking is one of the weaknesses in the ISIS policies. Not only are many civilians addicted to nicotine, this also goes for many fighters. The first cracks in the strict rules are visible. If ISIS guards catch a smuggler with cigarettes, there is a good chance that he will be able to convince them to take a share of the goods in return for his freedom, as is clear from stories from the area around Mosul that the Kurdish Peshmerga managed to liberate in early 2015. By these kinds of shady dealings, the supply has increased and the prices have dropped drastically.

Mosul Eye, a blogger who anonymously reports from the city, states that ISIS has started taxing civilians even more. On top of the monthly tax of 25,000 dinar (€17/$21), every household must now also pay a daily tax of 2,000 dinar (€1.45/$1.70) for 'services' despite there often being no electricity or water available.

And this in a city where the summer temperatures can reach 50 degrees Celsius (122 degrees Fahrenheit) – which means no air conditioning, no fans, no refrigerators, no cold water to drink and no showers.

Old houses in the city have deep, cool basements where my friend from Mosul as a child would spend the hottest part of the day having a siesta with the entire family – I would not be surprised if this habit has been reintroduced.

The tax system forces civilians to generate income. Until the government in Baghdad put an end to it in mid-2015, many still received their government salaries and were told to hand over a share to ISIS. Because many shortages arise due to closed transport routes, old smuggling routes are now once again in use. ISIS does not mind smuggling, as long as you pay up. Ali knows from his cousin that all merchants must make daily payments of 5 percent of their estimated profits. Every morning, taxi drivers must pay 5,000 dinars (€3.67/$4.29) in order to be permitted to work.

ISIS fighters are paid from the tax revenues, and this is partly why it is nearly impossible for citizens to leave the city. It is only permitted under very exceptional circumstances, and if you fail to return within fifteen days, the house and car you had to hand over as a guarantee, will be seized. If you do not own any property of value, you need to find someone who is willing to be you guarantor, who will end up in prison if you fail to report back. 'How will we get our money if we let them go?' an ISIS fighter asked Mosul Eye.

When a young man who needed a heart operation

outside the caliphate did not return in time, his entire family plus the man serving as his guarantor is said to have been executed by ISIS. This report cannot be authenticated, but even if it is incorrect, it still is effective as it feeds the fear of the residents.

Not everyone is given permission to leave the caliphate. Adnan, an activist from Raqqa, tried to have his aunt, who had cancer, receive treatment in Turkey. Although she had filled out the required papers and had property to leave behind as a guarantee, she was told to instead go for treatment in Mosul, for which ISIS paid the trip and part of the medical costs.

≈≈≈

Communication is difficult with people inside the caliphate. Initially, one could still phone with Mosul, but since the end of 2014, there is no longer any mobile network available. And yet people there still manage to communicate with the outside world via voice messages on WhatsApp, or they ride to the outskirts of the city to pick up an available network there. This is illegal however, because ISIS is afraid citizens will give information to the Americans, and their partners which could help them determine locations for their air strikes. This paranoia of course has great repercussions for the city. Everyone can be a spy. People have been executed due to those suspicions. This is why many residents are fearful to undertake any action. They know all too well that ISIS has many informants and that her revenge is bloody.

≈≈≈

In September of 2015, ISIS announces that in the period of one year more than 2,000 people have been executed in Mosul. At least, that is the number of names on the lists which have been pasted to the city walls. Shortly afterwards, the group tries some two hundred former police officers – including a nephew of my good friend from Mosul. His family is given back the body to bury, with two bullet holes in the head. Many others wait in vain for the remains of their loved ones. Rumors circulate in Mosul that this is because ISIS also executes people by driving them over with a heavy vehicle, and by pulling them apart while tied between two cars.

Among the victims are approximately three hundred civil servants who were involved with organizing the Iraqi elections in April of 2014, the majority being women. Many people are still missing, and are not on the ISIS lists so the number of those executed in Mosul is definitely higher than 2,000.

ISIS appears to operate from the mindset that people who are in doubt about the fate of their loved ones still have some hope, and will therefore abstain from resistance, while family members whose father or son has been murdered have nothing else to lose. They have become unreliable citizens, with some grasping every opportunity for resistance. But at the same time, the executions are for ISIS necessary as a tool to inflict fear on the population. It is all about finding a balance: enough executions to intimidate, but not enough to cause an uprising.

There are public executions every Friday. From people who spied, to those who spoke out against ISIS and still others accused of blasphemy or sorcery. Homosexuals are thrown from high buildings and adulterous men and women are stoned to death. Also doctors who refuse to go to the frontlines to care for ISIS fighters, and male doctors who treated women despite the ban are killed.

After the last of ISIS' strongholds in Iraq is liberated in 2017, dozens of mass graves are discovered; one of them in a huge sink hole outside Mosul. By mid-2018, still many of those arrested by ISIS remain missing.

Citizens are expected to watch the executions, as well as to go out on the streets in case of a military parade. They grumble about this amongst themselves, but they still go. Just like when they are forced to pray on the street, if they are outside during the call to prayer. Most of the people are afraid of the ISIS supporters who are controlling their lives, and who have changed their city into a prison.

≈ ≈ ≈

Prison, that's the word I get to hear too, when I ask around about the influence of ISIS on the lives of women in Mosul. Like from a young woman who via her Aunt Kifah in Erbil wants to tell me about the daily life. The conversation is conducted via WhatsApp.

'What has changed for women in Mosul under Daesh? Everything! Our freedom is their prisoner, in every sense of the word.' Then the power goes off in Mosul. 'I talk to my girlfriends and family all of the time via internet,' Kifah says, who herself fled soon after the arrival of ISIS with her husband and children to the Kurdistan region. 'Sometimes I sit and cry about what I am hearing.' Women barely leave their homes any more, she tells me. Because that is only permitted if they are dressed according to the regulations, and are accompanied by a male family member or their husband, who furthermore is registered in such a way by ISIS. Dashing out to do some quick shopping or visiting a girlfriend, now belongs to the past. During the Ramadan, women are even forbidden from showing themselves outside during the day.

The control is strict, as one of Kifah's girlfriends discovered when she went out with her family for a picnic on a spring day. In order to eat, she had to lift her niqaab. She was caught in the act by an overzealous ISIS supporter, who immediately punished her husband with lashes from a stick. That was the end of the picnic, also for others who had witnessed the incident and decided to head home.

With a burqa, public life has become absolutely impossible. You cannot even take a drink of water without lifting up the entire garment. The clothing rules have now in fact ensured that women no longer may eat or drink in public.

Even the hosing down of the sidewalk – a popular pastime for women in Iraq, whereby they can see what is going on in the street and talk with their neighbors – in Mosul is no longer what it was. As it is no longer permitted in a simple dress and while wearing slippers, and the woman may no longer stand outside alone; a male family member or her husband must keep her company.

Whoever is caught in the bazaar wearing only a headscarf instead of the niqaab or burqa, is sure to be punished by the Khansa brigade. Amongst them are armed Syrian women using a board with a nail sticking out of it, to injure women who do not adhere to the clothing rules.

After the liberation, women confirm the story that had already surfaced but was mostly considered too horrible to be true, that the Khansa brigade was also using the so-called biter to punish women. This metal instrument was used to bite into the flesh and left terrible wounds.

Before the arrival of ISIS, Mosul already was a city where strict Muslims lived. But there was an abundance of women's hairdressers, just like shops selling makeup and lingerie. They have all now shut down, under the threat that they would otherwise be burnt down. The hairdresser now comes to your home or works secretly from her own home. The mannequins in the shops are now veiled or without a head. There is hardly any choice in the type of clothing, and cheerful fabrics are out. Anything else, one can only buy illegally. Beneath the counter, for example – and that is true as well for lingerie. All types of clothing are now being sold in people's homes, and there is a lively exchange of clothes taking place.

Shopping, much more of a hobby for women in Iraq than in the West, no longer exists. Women only go outside when it is absolutely necessary, for a doctor's appointment for example. The shopping is done by men and elderly women, for whom the mandatory niqaab is less strict; they are permitted to go out wearing a headscarf, Kifah says, despite this being in contradiction with the reports from escaped members of the Khansa brigade from Raqqa about older women being beaten for a violation of the clothing rules. This can be caused by the fact that Mosul is known as being a difficult city to control, as the Americans discovered following the invasion in 2003, when an armed resistance soon turned the city against them.

In any case, in the caliphate women no longer have a role in public life. Girls still may go to elementary school, but not high school and certainly not to university. By the summer of 2016, ISIS has closed most schools to be used for storing weapons.

A young woman in Mosul whom I contacted by WhatsApp, complains about the lack of a social life. 'We live in a time when you hear no news from others.' And due to the limitations placed on education, ISIS has destroyed her future, she says.

The rules of ISIS also have consequences for the health care for women. Not only are they barred from visiting male doctors, ISIS has also forbidden the caesarean section, which is more normal in Iraq than in the West. According to ISIS, women must suffer during their delivery, Kifah heard from her friends. Female doctors protested, and eventually succeeded in being allowed to perform the operation still in cases of emergency.

≈ ≈ ≈

The fear for ISIS dominates the entire life. A girlfriend of Kifah had gone up onto the flat roof of her house to find a better signal to communicate with her family via WhatsApp. When she saw the black flag of ISIS waving on top of a nearby roof, she made it off the roof as quickly as she could. 'As if the flag could see and snitch on her,' Kifah says grinning.

Next to all of this, a lack of money has forced many men to join ISIS, in order to support their families. The decision is one borne usually from desperation. The order of the tribes is strong in Mosul; and if a tribal chief joins ISIS, this means that the organization will also be getting the rest of the tribe.

A woman can often do little else than accept the fact that her husband is collaborating with ISIS, even if she is against it. Most women have no choice, Kifah says. 'They are afraid to leave their husband, because usually the entire family has joined Daesh.'

According to a member of the action group DeirEzzor24, which reports on the situation in the Syrian ISIS-city Deir al-Zour, a cousin who joined ISIS receives 100 dollars per month (€86). Plus an extra 100 dollars for his parents and $40 (€34) more for each of his brothers and sisters. In this way, ISIS binds the entire family to them. 'The policy of Daesh is to starve people, while the fighters are being paid. The only way to survive is to join Daesh,' according to an activist who operates outside of the caliphate. And 'the only good job is a job with ISIS,' a member of the action groups Raqqa is being slaughtered silently says. Approximately sixty percent of the Syrians are unemployed. In Raqqa, this is why some citizens rent their homes to ISIS fighters, or work in the religious schools of ISIS.

Abu Bakr al-Baghdadi has repeatedly called on Muslims to join him. Then they will no longer be 'homeless' and 'humiliated,' because citizens in the caliphate live 'with power and honor' and 'are certain of God's gifts.' ISIS does indeed reward its supporters.

Kifah from Mosul, knows a family who after joining ISIS could trade their meagre home in Mosul for a house that had been seized from fleeing Christians. For that reason, a daughter and son-in-law refused to move into that house, and stood their ground despite being threatened – but they are without doubt an exception.

Hardly anyone dares to protest against ISIS. The group tolerates no one who resists them, or could do so in the future. That is clear from the story of human rights activist Buthaina al-Jibouri from Eski Mosul, a village located just outside Mosul with some 9,000 residents, which was occupied by ISIS for seven months. After the liberation, her husband, Sheik Abdullah Ibrahim al-Jibouri told The Associated Press ISIS had demanded that she officially would have to 'repent' before one of the ISIS courts, because she had been candidate on multiple occasions for the provincial council of Mosul.

He knew the refusal from his wife would cost her

dearly. The sheik had seen how police officers in the village had been shot dead for the same reason. He therefore sent her away. But a few days later, she was back; she could not stand being away from her five children, with the youngest son of two still taking the breast. After some time, a group of ISIS men came to their house to take her away. The sheik went to see one of the highest ISIS officials to plead her case.

Despite his belonging to one of the most influential tribes and his telling them that his wife was still breastfeeding the youngest, he achieved nothing. 'What difference does it make? Your children will be orphans,' he was told. Shortly afterwards he received the death certificate of his wife, with at the top the black ISIS logo.

Little is known about the treatment of women in the ISIS prisons, probably because the women who end up there never make it back out alive. From the men who have managed to survive, we do know the system differs little from that of the Iraqi and Syrian dictators Saddam and Assad, with abuse, hard-handed interrogations and torture. It is said that for female prisoners, their hair is completely shaved off before they are executed: stoning in case of adultery, shot to death in other cases. The hair of a woman is seen as one of her most attractive characteristics throughout the entire region.

Even a minor crime or the conviction that you are not religious enough, can cost you your life. People disappear, and their families receive in the best case scenario a death certificate, sometimes a video of the decapitation, but sometimes also nothing.

Papers are important in the caliphate. Former police officers for instance must voice regret over their former lives and hand over their service weapons, and in return receive a document which they must carry with them at all times. Many have therefore had the paper sealed in plastic. The same rules pertain to English teachers, who give lessons in a 'forbidden' language, and from tailors who have at any stage made clothing which was not Islamic. Whoever fails to carry that document, can be arrested by one of the Hisba patrols, the male version of the Khansa brigade. People prefer to remain at home, just to avoid contact with them, and often avoid the checkpoints of the Hisba.

Hisba members drive around in SUV's with tinted windows. They wear a balaclava or a scarf across their face. Because they believe that they are unrecognizable, they feel free to abuse their power. In the best case scenario, they will issue a fine or a prison sentence of a few hours or days. But sometimes, they tie offenders to a pole on the square for days, with a sign hanging around their neck listing their offence.

The foreign women of the Khansa brigade are darlings compared to the members of the Hisba, as is clear from an incident in the Syrian city of Muhassan, where a Hisba member reprimands a woman sweeping her stoop as she is not sufficiently covered. When her brother protests, this leads to a fight. The militant then shoots and kills the brother. Then he is shot himself by the other brothers. ISIS takes revenge and sends a unit to the house, and kills all eight members of the family.

This kind of excessive violence paralyzes the citizens, while in the meantime the rules are continually being tightened. Every time new ones are added, and announced in the mosque and by flyers. This way, it is also made known that it is no longer permitted to mourn at the grave of the deceased. ISIS places this under the ban that prohibits praying at the grave of a saint. The Hisba sends grieving family members away, due to forbidden 'worshipping of graves' and punishes all who protest this.

Only ISIS fighters and officials have freedoms. Just like in Raqqa, ISIS fighters and officials in Mosul also have the best homes. ISIS gave homes left empty for months by Christians mainly to the foreign fighters. In Mosul, half of the ISIS corps is said to be made up of foreigners, with the rest being Iraqis from elsewhere, mostly from the villages. Especially supporters from the neighboring Talafar, the so-called Afari, are notorious for their violent behavior. 'There is not a single honorable Maslawi with Daesh,' says the young woman in Mosul whom I speak to via WhatsApp, using the local name for residents of

Mosul. 'People must know that Daesh has distanced itself from the true and peaceful Islam. Daesh has come to destroy, to kill and to plunder. The Maslawi's will have nothing to do with them.' Western ISIS fighters form a separate class in the society of ISIS, and they barely mingle with the original residents living under occupation.

≈≈≈

Because Mosul was a mixed city up until the arrival of ISIS, it was normal that not everyone participated in the fasting during the Ramadan. Furthermore, there are also numerous reasons why Muslims do not have to fast, for example in case of illness, menstruation or because they are travelling. But now, it is mandatory for everyone over twelve years of age, and ISIS locks those up in a cage who are caught eating or drinking – and just remember how hot it is. There, they are publicly humiliated for hours. Sources in Syria report that ISIS chastises the people there who do not observe the Ramadan, or even publicly crucifies them on a cross.

All of the festivities which give the month of fasting its special character, have been cancelled under ISIS. Previously, families would visit one another after sunset to break the fast together, and in the evenings the cafes were busy, as backgammon was played and water pipes smoked. Next to smoking, games are now also forbidden. In the Iraqi city of Fallujah, which has been in the hands of ISIS since early 2014 (and will remain until June 2016), men may no longer congregate in the tea houses following the Iftar, the meal which breaks the fast once the sun has gone down. There is also an extra clothing rule for men during the Ramadan: no short sleeves or shorts.

≈≈≈

Civilians in the occupied cities are aware of the fate of the Yazidi women ISIS has kidnapped. Kifah tells me that initially, the trade in Yazidi girls happened openly in the streets of Mosul. She heard from one of her friends how ISIS supporters would unload the women from a truck, and have them cross the road and into a park. Their clothes were partially ripped off to reveal more of their bodies to the eager male buyers. From her story it also becomes obvious, that many civilians who try to survive under ISIS, have chosen the side of the Yazidi women, because they are proud of Mosul and Raqqa as multi-ethnic societies of Sunnis, Shiites, Christians and Yazidis living together.

Some stories really touched me deeply. In the hospital where a friend of Kifah works, a Yazidi women was brought in who had suffered a miscarriage. Doctors and nurses begged the man who had brought her in to allow her to stay there until the anesthesia had worn off. But he refused, and dragged the woman out of the hospital. The same happened with a ten-year-old girl who had been brought in with serious injuries as the result of repeated rapes. Her situation brought the doctors who were treating her to tears, and they begged the ISIS men to leave the child behind, because she needed much more medical care. But they simply refused.

≈ ≈ ≈

Mosul also had to deal with brothels using Yazidi girls; and this must have been the same in other cities. In the neighborhood of the air force base in Mosul, many homes from former air force personnel were confiscated by ISIS. And there, in the middle of a residential neighborhood, the brothels are now located. Those living there are often startled at night by the screams of the women.

Residents can only help those women who run away from the brothels and out of the homes of ISIS supporters. In numerous cases, neighbors have given escaped Yazidi women shelter and helped them to flee from the city. Also money is being raised to buy the girls' freedom, Kifah tells me. Her husband is involved in this. Once they have been bought, they are smuggled out of the city.

With every step taken, ISIS tries to convince the

population that what it is doing is in accordance with Islam. Instead, for many residents this only confirms how ISIS abuses Islam, but they can only talk about this in their homes and without the children being present, as ISIS uses them to spy and report.

This is only one of many reasons, why women are concerned about their children. In the changed school system, the boys are now indoctrinated and prepared for a job within ISIS, or to go and fight on the frontline. Keeping boys at home is not allowed, neither is preventing them from going to the war.

The result of the indoctrination could be heard from civilians fleeing from the Syrian city Tal Abyad to Turkey, after the Kurds had taken the city. In a conversation with journalists, teen-aged boys from the town highly praised ISIS. 'The Islamic State is the best. There is no better life. Everything happens under the laws of Allah. Safety is the most important thing, and we had that. There were no thieves. Before they came, we had forgotten the real Islam. These people have shown us the right path.'

When in 2016 ISIS is losing more and more ground and fighters, the group starts using more of the children that have been trained in its special training camps. Not only at the frontline, where according to some sources at least half of the fighters are now under eighteen years of age, but also in suicide missions. In August 2016, a fifteen-year-old boy is caught before he manages to explode his suicide vest in a Shiite mosque in Kirkuk, as moments later another boy of around the same age does succeed to blow himself up elsewhere in the city. Just days before, a boy who mingled amongst the youth at a wedding in the Turkish city of Gaziantep exploded his vest, and in March 2016 another one did so at a youth football match in the south of Iraq. Judging from the pictures ISIS posts on social media, many of the suicide bombers that drive their trucks laden with explosives into the Kurdish Peshmerga at the frontline, are also kids.

Days after the boy in Kirkuk is caught, ISIS posts a video on social media showing the killing of prisoners by five boys. Clad in military fatigues, with a black cap over their hair but their faces free, they shoot five men in orange jumpsuits by pistol. These are Kurds captured three years before in Syria, while one of the adolescent killers is a Kurd himself. The others appear to be children of foreign fighters; one British, another Tunisian, yet another Egyptian and the last one Uzbek, all nationalities of men who joined ISIS from abroad.

In an effort to prevent their children from being brainwashed, parents keep them home from the schools and Mosul University, which according to the blogger Mosul Eye has resulted in the latter being transformed into a kind of ghost town.

During Saddam Hussein's rule and even afterwards, the university was regarded as one of the best in Iraq. But now, there are barely any students. ISIS starts using the grounds more and more to store weapons, make explosive devises and even develop chemical weapons, until the Americans bombed the sites in March 2016.

When parents start to keep their daughters home from the elementary schools, ISIS initially thinks that this is due to normal absenteeism. But when the numbers continue to increase and they fail to return, it becomes clear that it is a form of protest, according to the blogger.

Another reason to keep their daughters home, is the rumor that ISIS fighters go to the schools and choose the prettiest girls, and force them into marriage. Whether the rumor is indeed based upon fact, is impossible to confirm, even after the liberation.

Children too cannot avoid the strict punishments in the caliphate. A video of a father from Mosul has emerged, in which he pleads to the Hisba for his ten-year-old son. The child has stolen food, which is understandable given the shortages. In the video can be seen, how the boy is executed by a shot to the back of his head. Witnesses also report that in a separate incident, four children of eleven, twelve, thirteen and sixteen years old, who had been caught committing petty thefts, all lost a hand.

≈ ≈ ≈

In Raqqa, the feeling of powerlessness is no less than in Mosul. 'The people hate ISIS, but they are desperate and expect no support if they should revolt against them,' Raqqa activist Adnan states to the Associated Press in June of 2015. 'They feel abandoned.' The 28-year-old Adnan has seen how Raqqa changed under ISIS. Not only the clothing for the women, the praying in the streets and the empty tea houses, but also the use of the soccer stadium as a prison – renamed Point 11 – and the executions on one of the central squares, which people now call the Square from Hell. Bodies are left hanging there for three days.

He describes how ISIS tightened the net for the residents, after it had taken over various cities in Syria. After first killing the police officers and soldiers, others were given the opportunity to repent by literally paying off their past, sometimes for as much as thousands of dollars. ISIS tried to win support from civilians by offering water, electricity and petrol for free and by digging sewers. After this, stricter rules were announced. Civilians were ordered to build walls around their houses, so the women would remain unseen. Pharmacists were given a course in Sharia law and were no longer permitted to sell contraceptives. In every neighborhood, ISIS appointed an emir as the local manager. Local families or tribes were given jobs and privileges in return for their loyalty to ISIS. Land and property from those who had fled, was confiscated. Trade within the caliphate – for example cement, fruit and vegetables from Turkey via Raqqa to Mosul – was stimulated, because it generated tax revenue.

There are rules, rules and more rules. Some seem trivial, such as the ban of tuning your radio in on another station than the ISIS one with quotes from the Quran, and the ban on fishing with dynamite. Still others reveal that there are indeed people working for ISIS who realize what is expected from a state; such as the control in shops on food which has passed the expiration date, and in slaughterhouses for sick animals. Sometimes, it became clear that there were people at the top who understood how to capture the hearts and minds. For example, at the reopening of a luxury hotel on the banks of the Tigris in Mosul, all newlywed couples were offered a free honeymoon there for three nights.

Even though it does eventually happen, it is hard to imagine ISIS gone. Like a painter in Raqqa who earns a good living painting its offices in Raqqa puts it: 'People are now used to this way of life.' Safety and stability, that is what most people long for, and that is what ISIS gives them. Many have, just as ISIS had planned, become dependent on its services.

Also the views of people have changed. A resident from Raqqa told The New York Times: 'If you had asked me before the revolution, I would have said that I wanted to be rich, with houses and cars. But now that we have sat with their religious teachers, our manner of thinking has changed.' He also said, he is considering joining ISIS, and is convinced he will marry in Raqqa and raise his children there, so that they will learn the 'true religion'.

≈ ≈ ≈

The position of women in this process is not entirely clear. The women I speak to, are against ISIS, but that cannot be true for everyone. There are women who, just like the man in Raqqa, have allowed themselves to be persuaded, and perhaps especially by their husbands.

In Raqqa, ISIS wanted local women to marry the fighters. Here, it is still customary that cousins marry one another, and so most of the parents refused to cooperate. But according to Raqqa is being slaughtered silently, ISIS increased the pressure by harassing the young women in the streets. Rumors about kidnappings were circulating, with a marriage as the only remedy against possible shame. Moreover, ISIS offered high dowries and an abundance of advantages for families who agreed to bonding with the group in this manner. According to the action group, a number of women who had been promised to an ISIS fighter, committed suicide. Besides this, the group reports that women who marry foreign fighters may end up in a judicial vacuum, because they usually only know his nickname. This has consequences for possibly children, especially if the fighter is killed. And if he moves along with the frontline, and leaves behind his wife in Raqqa, he will often take a second wife at the new location.

In June of 2015, reports are heard from Mosul that at least ninety young women had been taken from their homes by the Khansa brigade, because they refused to agree to a marriage proposal. They were expected to make themselves available for a jihad al-nikah, a marriage as a holy war. Kurdish media in Iraq report that they were forced to marry fighters. These reports cannot be confirmed; this can be anti-ISIS propaganda which ISIS uses themselves to instill fear amongst the people.

≈ ≈ ≈

The war is having ever-greater consequences for the civilian population in the occupied cities. The Americans and their coalition partners bomb targets on a daily basis, often also in the cities, sometimes even in residential areas. That is where for instance the seized houses of the civilians who fled are located, that ISIS now uses as storages facilities for explosives. After an air strike on one of these, in which an entire family was killed, the neighbors of other storage facilities immediately decided to move away.

When in July of 2015, the Americans again drop pamphlets above Mosul which announce the upcoming liberation of the city, hundreds of families manage to leave, and via Syria and Turkey eventually reach the Kurdish region of Iraq. They had likely hired smugglers, just like the Syrian activist Adnan, who as he flees from Raqqa, first is taken to the border crossing at Tal Abyad, and from there across the Turkish border. Human traffickers have been active in the region for decades. Besides this, having wasta, so the right connections, is just as defining as elsewhere in the Middle East, as the story of a 63-year-old shop owner from Al-Zaab, near Mosul illustrates. He succeeded in convincing the authorities that he had to travel for three days for his work. He was given a paper, without having to pay a deposit or sign anything. He left with his wife, son and daughter-in-law, but was stopped at the second checkpoint. The guards there, decided that his car had not been registered properly, and that also the usual paper which served as proof of the payment of a deposit was absent. 'That is punishable by execution,' he was told.

But then a commander at the checkpoint made a call, and suddenly the family was allowed to pass. The only reason why that could have happened, is that the shop keeper knew the commander, who himself knew someone in the right position in the ISIS machinery. The difference between having the right contact and having none, can be the one between life and death.

By the spring of 2016, ISIS has lost almost 50 percent of its territory in Iraq, and some important routes between its cities. In August 2016, Washington reports that the ongoing battle has cost at least 45,000 ISIS fighters their lives, with only about 15,000 of them left. After the liberation of Mosul, and most of Iraq in 2017, the Americans put the number of ISIS fighters killed at 60.000 to 70.000.

≈≈≈

With the battle raging, the situation in villages and cities under ISIS control steadily deteriorated, as I hear from villagers who manage to flee, when the battle reaches their areas in the summer of 2016. Impoverished, left with no money for all the taxes ISIS has been demanding, hungry, stuck in their houses for fear of being picked up and executed for minor offenses, the women throw off their black burqas as soon as they reach safety.

Meanwhile, the oppression is worse than ever. This explains reports from Mosul about limited resistance; snipers have taken aim at high-ranking ISIS officials, their homes have been burned, and members of the Hisba and the Khansa brigade have been murdered. People paint an 'M' on walls, short for Muqawama, or resistance in Arabic. It also gets sprayed on houses where ISIS fighters or leaders live, who often flee once they discover it, fearing it might mean they are going to be targeted by coalition air strikes. Informants relay possible targets to the Americans. To prevent the latter from happening, ISIS has registered all internet users.

Various sources in Mosul conclude, the situation would have been different if the Iraqi army had not disarmed them before the arrival of ISIS. Out of fear that the population would join the radical group if and when it attempted to take over control of the city, the army had ordered civilians to surrender all of their weapons. 'With only a few knives, we cannot do much against ISIS,' they say.

Even so, the blogger Mosul Eye in the summer of 2015 shows to be convinced that the residents of Mosul know that ISIS cannot not stay forever and will eventually leave. And that they will say: 'This is our city, and we are not leaving. ISIS is the one who has to go.'

9
AFTER ISIS

Is there a life after ISIS? For the kidnapped Yazidi women? For the recruits who discovered that they had made a mistake? For the civilians in the occupied cities? The indoctrinated young people?

Four years after their kidnapping from the Sinjar region by ISIS, around 3,300 Yazidis were freed, about half of them women. About 3,100 women and children were still kept in captivity, all of the women as sex slaves.

I have talked to many women after their return from the caliphate; nearly all of them are traumatized. This is why the role of the spiritual leader of the Yazidis, the Baba Sheik, is so important. I have visited the friendly 81-year-old leader several times in his centuries-old residence in Sheikhan, where in the shade of the courtyard men seated on plastic chairs drink tea and talk, while visitors mingle with the clergymen, who are recognizable by their long, white robes.

'We call on the community to welcome the returning women without any reservations, and to accept them as normal marital partners,' he says in a discussion we have at the end of August of 2014. It is stated exactly the same way in the official message he sends out shortly afterwards in several languages. In a reaction to this, Yazidi youths declare that they will marry these girls if they are ever freed.

There are strict rules governing the Yazidis. Whoever marries outside the group is ostracized from it. Just like those who convert to another faith. The community can only grow from the inside, because you are only born as a Yazidi and cannot convert to it. But because the survival of the group is in danger, the strict Yazidi law has been liberalized. The Baba Sheik tells me that he promises clemency for those who were forced to convert to Islam. 'If they had no choice, we will welcome them back into our midst. They may not be blamed for the loss of their honor, nor for converting under force.'

The strict rules are connected to the history of the Yazidis, in which rulers time and again forced them to convert. Also, the stealing of women is a returning theme during the 73 previous attacks, which the Yazidis have listed as genocide in their history books. In the nineteenth century, a Kurdish tribal chief kidnapped thousands of women and forced them to marry members of his tribe, hundreds of kilometers from home.

≈ ≈ ≈

I have become friends with the much younger half-brother of the spiritual leader, Hadi Babasheik, who has lived in Germany for many years, where there is a large Yazidi community. We can therefore talk without an official translator being present. Sometimes he accompanies me on visits to the camps near Sheikhan, and via Viber we share stories about the escaped women.

We speak about the dilemma, that as a result of the atrocities by ISIS, followed by a stay in refugee camps and desperation of their situation, many Yazidis want to leave Iraq. Some borrow money and let themselves be taken to Europe by human traffickers, and many end up stranded in Turkey and Bulgaria, and later in Greece. Hadi Babasheik emphasizes the preference of the spiritual leader, that his people remain in Iraq, because once abroad the Yazidis will be lost for the community due to their marriages to people from the local population.

The Yazidi community has already shrunk considerably, to at the most 650,000 in Iraq and another estimated 100,000 faithful spread across the globe.

Although some 150 girls in ISIS captivity committed suicide, the promise from Baba Sheik clearly had an effect, as it reached the kidnapped women and inspired them to escape. A number of them were able to phone, often in the middle of the night, with confidants in the Yazidi community in Kurdistan, including my friend and colleague Khidher Domle. He has sacrificed countless night's sleep for these painful conversations. His role was a supportive one, a listening ear, sometimes as a middleman in helping to arrange their escape. He always consoled the women: if you get back here, no one will blame you for anything.

Most of the women were without too much ado accepted back into the community. Unfortunately, some women's organizations have claimed the exact opposite, probably in an effort not to disappoint their financial backers. A Kurdish blogger reports that an uncle threatened to kill his pregnant and desperate niece if it turned out she had lost her honor to ISIS. But I rely on the aid workers I speak to, and from them I only hear about isolated incidents of returning girls having these kinds of problems.

For the women who do return, a visit to the Yazidi holy place of Lalesh is essential, where they undergo a cleansing ritual. This little village located in green mountains, where the sanctity of the place demands that you walk on bare feet, has a temple which enters into an underground cave. There is a holy well, in which children are baptized and the returning women are cleansed. This ritual is for most women the confirmation that despite of everything that has happened, they are being accepted back into the community.

≈≈≈

The Dutch-Kurdish psychiatrist and sexologist Bayan Rasul says that she contacted not only the Baba Sheik, but also the Kurdish government in the first days after the kidnappings, to convince them to release a statement that the women were welcome. 'I am very happy that it worked.' I know Rasul well and have often spoken to her about her medical specialties. This time, I go to see her, hoping to be able to better understand the psychological circumstances of the escaped women. We meet for a tea in one of the most expensive hotels in Erbil, repeatedly interrupted by politicians and dignitaries who greet us.

Rasul is driven. Not only has she taken on the task of the psychological treatment for Yazidi women, she even confronted Kurdish Prime Minister Nechirvan Barzani with her concerns about the fact that the escaped Yazidi women were being questioned by the security police, the assaish, after arriving in Kurdistan. She pointed out to him that the incriminating conversations with women who had been abused and raped by men, were being conducted by male officers. 'We have asked for female assaish, but there are none. There is also no understanding for our request,' she sighs.

That nearly all of the women who managed to escaped are traumatized, doesn't need the eye of an expert. That the one is worse off than the other is clear too. Rasul explains to me that the situation varies from person to person. 'Many deny what has happened, do not want to believe it, tell themselves that it was just a dream. That often comes after a period of shock, a kind of freezing, but it can also happen the other way around. Then there are symptoms of stress: they cannot sleep, are afraid, are unable to enjoy anything, have flashbacks, nightmares, they relive it all over again.' According to Rasul, this is the acute phase, which can last for up to six months. 'That is normal.' Even without treatment, all this will eventually diminish, but it is very possible that much later on – sometimes even after twenty years – suddenly it will return with extreme stress and fear. Then treatment is still necessary.

A huge problem in Iraq is the taboo for getting any psychological help. 'Many people do not want to be treated, because they aren't crazy! We have had to come up with other terminology; we call it education, a focus group, handicraft or sewing lessons, a training about opening your own business...'

I ask Rasul why Smile made such an impression on me. 'That smile is a mask, because people talk about her behind her back. She doesn't want them to know it bothers her.'

Rasul blames the camouflaged language used by the women, for example speaking of 'marriage' while they are talking about being raped, mainly on shame. That is why during treatment, they should first of all change the image they have of themselves. 'The women often do not know what happens in a war. I tell them that they are the victim of war crimes. In doing so, I can slowly give them back their self-respect.' According to Rasul, treatment is in any case a necessity. 'Otherwise they will never be able to enjoy life, will have physical complaints, no appetite for food, or an excessive appetite which then results in obesity, and concentration problems. The body breaks down due to the high levels of the stress hormone cortisol. Then there is the social life: they no longer trust anyone. And if they are married, they can no longer make any contact with their own husband.'

The problem is that Iraq and Iraqi Kurdistan hardly have psychotherapists and psychiatrists who can offer the correct therapy. The majority of Kurdish psychiatrists only prescribe medication. The number of psychotherapists with clinical experience is small, because of unavailability of good educational programs. In the meantime, the number of patients has grown enormously: many thousands, because one should also include Yazidis who were left traumatized from fleeing for the fighters of ISIS in August of 2014.

In the Netherlands, group therapy would be the solution, Rasul says. 'Things go faster in a group, but our culture of shame is not suitable for that. No one wants it. That is why we often resort to painting with a group or handcrafts, and talk all the while about how life was 'there'. Often they will then tell about their own pain through the story of another.'

I heard numerous women complaining that they are fainting repeatedly. Rasul speaks of 'pseudo-epilepsy, a psychosomatic complaint, when what has happened is too bad to experience consciously. It is a form of self-protection. Some have a dissociative disorder: they turn away from the conscious and see themselves sitting there.'

Her male colleague, the psychiatrist Fatih Faiz has an extreme example of the latter. 'I have a patient who so vividly relived what happened to her, that she put her own hands around her throat because she had nearly been strangled by someone.' He is involved in a project for treating the thousands of victims of ISIS, including women and children, in Germany. Faiz says that some of the women are afraid of all men. 'They panicked when they met a small group of older Yazidis in Germany. They were Yazidis, but they all had long beards and that caused the bad memories to resurface.'

≈≈≈

In a clinic in the refugee camp by Khanke, with some 30,000 Yazidis, the Jiyan Foundation offers help to traumatized women. It is an organization for mental health with several branches in Kurdistan. One of the psychiatrists is Wahid Ablaod Harmz. As Yazidi women also do not report to him with their traumas, the Christian doctor who received his education in Sweden therefore offers all forms of medical help, in an effort to get the women at least to come in during the consultation hours. When I visit him in the white mobile office, the waiting room is filled with women of all ages and their children. Fifty patients report here daily, Harmz says. They come for the female family doctor, and then Harmz gets to work with patients that he recognizes as having psychosomatic complaints. 'Small pains, often in the stomach and intestines. Some also come with depression, and then bit by bit tell me more'.

During a round through the small clinic, he surprises two young sisters, sitting across from a young psychologist in training. He is conducting the intake consultation with the oldest, because she keeps fainting, her sister tells us obediently. I feel like an intruder, but Harmz insists that we have our picture taken together. The sisters smile timidly.

Just like Bayan Rasul, this doctor works on the rehabilitation of the women's self-respect. He tells them about his own background; during the rule of Saddam Hussein he spent five years in one of the cruelest prisons of Iraq, Abu Ghraib. 'I tell them that I was afraid of sexual abuse there, but also that the worth of a person is not tied to that one part of our bodies. That they must accept what has happened, because it was not their choice: it was done to them. And that they should be proud of themselves because they survived it and have maintained their faith.'

After twenty sessions the women usually feel better. Harmz would also like to treat their family members to increase the chance of recovery, 'but it is difficult to reach the men. They feel so much shame for what happened to their women.'

≈ ≈ ≈

For Sherri Kraham, those men are also an issue. This American woman, who has worked at the American Ministry of Foreign Affairs, married the son of an important politician in Iraqi Kurdistan. While her husband, Qubad Talabani, climbed to the post of deputy prime minister, she did not allow herself to be pushed into the constraints of being 'the wife of'. With a girlfriend she established – thanks to donations and not with governmental funding, as she stresses – the Seed Foundation, which opened a women's center in the camp near Akre for the 13,000 Yazidis who were staying there until 2017. The center organized courses and other activities for women and children and there was a clinic, also for psychological help. 'We want offer a safe and warm environment,' Kraham says. An important element are the vegetable gardens, for the women to be 'active and productive.' Producing vegetables and fruit for the family, they once again feel valued. 'If they sit in their tent all day, they only relive their trauma,' Kraham concludes.

She came up with the idea because she had a vegetable garden herself. For the realization of the vegetable gardens and guiding the women there, she coincidentally chose one of my friends in Kurdistan, the Dutch agricultural engineer and former soccer international Annemiek van Waarden. She has grown fruit and potatoes and advised the Kurdish government how to develop the agriculture.

Kraham realizes that she should not exclude the men, especially because she wants to fight the domestic violence in the camp. 'If you want to limit the violence against women, you must do something for the men. I involve them by teaching them to make furniture from wooden pallets.'

Salah Ahmad, the director of the Jiyan Foundation, also has plans involving a garden. Germany is funding the trauma center in Chamchamal that he opened far from the Yazidi camps for traumatized Yazidi women, which contains a healing garden. In combination with therapy, the relaxation provided by nature and the care for the animals that live in the garden help the women to deal with their traumas in the relatively short period of time of three to six months.

With his hands, Ahmad draws the large center he eventually wants to establish for sixty to ninety women. Because the financing is not yet complete, he has started out smaller in a building lent to him by the government. He would prefer working with female therapists, but has no idea where to find them. In order to make a start, once again with German aid, he has given a group of psychologists a crash course. Others he hopes to give 'on the job training.'

≈≈≈

While speaking to these driven people, I discover that there is virtually no contact between them, while they do criticize one another. Wahid Ablaod Harmz for example, thinks it is unwise that his own director, Salam Ahmad, wants to treat women separately from men and family members.

They all are critical towards the transfer of women to Germany, an initiative which was borne from desperation at the beginning of 2015, when the Kurdish government saw no other alternative due to the lack of local specialists. Just over a thousand women and children went to Germany for two years, and most went on to apply for a residency permit afterwards. This is not wise, according to Harmz: 'They are not going to Germany for a treatment, but to get away from Iraq,' he believes. 'You must have a good understanding of the Yazidi culture in order to be able to treat them successfully,' he emphasizes.

His boss, Salah Ahmad agrees. 'They take a woman with these kinds of horrific experiences and who only speaks Kurdish, from primitive surroundings into a modern society. She cannot understand the people, nor the culture.' He furthermore points out that the costs for treatment in Germany are five times higher than in Kurdistan. Because Iraq has many more traumatized people as a result of all of the wars, it is far better to establish good local projects, he emphasizes time and again.

Furthermore, the risk for potential burnouts threatens therapists. The doctors confide in me, that hearing the gruesome stories is also a heavy burden for them. It exceeds all comprehension that people can do this to one another, one of them says. Due to the shortage of therapists they must treat many patients and can barely get any rest, which in the long term could well lead to problems.

By the time ISIS was evicted from Iraq in 2017,

more therapists had become available, partly thanks to a course started at the university of Koya, partly because of input from abroad, by way of more specialized training and coaching. But the situation remained critical; there still are by far not enough therapists and centers to provide the needed help, and I have met traumatized women who returned from ISIS after three or even four years who do not get the care they need.

≈≈≈

Men and boys who managed to flee from ISIS make up a minority in the group of the escapees. They are mainly children and teenagers, and a few elderly men. In the refugee camps, the men feel powerless and frustrated because they cannot care for their families, and many have great difficulty in accepting the kidnapping of their wives and daughters and the loss of family members. This leads to domestic violence, but that problem is surrounded by so much shame that it is hardly discussed; Kraham being a clear exception. In 2014, I tried to learn more about a UN report that was released following an investigation in the camps for Syrian refugees in Kurdistan. But it had quickly disappeared into a drawer, and none of the researchers were willing to elaborate on their findings.

With people unwilling to return to Sinjar after it

was liberated, the camps will most probably slowly transform into villages. Agricultural projects like Sherri Kraham's can contribute to this. The emergence of a local economy can help the men in regaining the direction of their own lives and in doing so also their sense of self-respect. But the realization that many also are in need of psychological help is virtually non-existent, not only for them but also in the outside world.

Happily, the awareness is there when it pertains to the children who have been indoctrinated and returned from the caliphate damaged. One of the women in this book, Khanu, tells me that her sons are unruly. 'The eldest listens to no one and the youngest wants to pray all the time, even when we tell him he no longer has to.' Experts on indoctrination have stated that deprogramming projects must be established for the children, but that these types of programs first need to be developed.

'Children are mainly afraid,' Bayan Rasul concludes. 'Some think: ISIS is still close by, so I had better be good.'

≈≈≈

In Erbil, Christian friends tell me about visits by evangelists to the Yazidis. They brought them bibles and promised that they could immigrate to America. Already 20,000 bibles were handed out and money was being raised in the United States for another 20,000 more – intended for people who have lost everything. On the site of the Christian Aid Mission, I read that the organization has converted nearly eight hundred displaced persons in the provinces of Erbil and Duhok, of whom two thirds are Yazidi. I share my indignation about this with friends: how can you take people who have escaped from the clutches of ISIS, and still want to convert them to yet another faith? These are people who would accept anything to get out of the misery, and who are traumatized and therefore incapable of making wise decisions.

The evangelists come up with the example of a fifteen-year-old shoe polisher, whose two sisters were kidnapped by ISIS. His father had become paralyzed because of this. The boy, who now had to support the entire family, had not eaten in four days. He took the evangelists to the tent where the family was living, after which they prayed with the father and a number of other family members. When they were told that Jesus heals, 'they opened their hearts immediately to the Lord.'

≈ ≈ ≈

Not only Yazidi children who managed to escape from ISIS are suffering from the consequences of indoctrination. The same is true for the children of local populations in the caliphate and in the cities where ISIS has been driven out. Just listen to the children who fled with their parents from the Syrian city Tal Abyad to Turkey, after the Kurds had retaken the city from ISIS. Lindsey Hilsum from the British Channel 4 spoke to a family with teenage sons who already appeared in chapter 7. They fanatically idolize Jihadi John, a British ISIS fighter who, before his death in a coalition attack, was notorious due to his role in the executions of Western hostages. He was their hero; they had seen him numerous times in Tal Abyad. 'He is famous!' the boys said.

'He is in Brigade Seventeen. He wore the same clothing as in the videos. [...] He was right to kill the journalists, because they were all spies who pretended to be journalists.' Hilsum writes that the teenagers eagerly explained that if you steal a bicycle on the street which is not locked, this is not a crime. But if you enter a house to steal, there is a punishment of amputation from the wrist for the first offense, from the elbow for the second, and from the shoulder if you are caught a third time, they said.

One of the boys, who had been to the headquarters of ISIS in Raqqa on a regular basis, told her he had seen how homosexuals were thrown from high buildings. 'It is exactly as in the time of the Prophet. Well, you didn't have tall buildings then, so they had to be thrown off a mountain.'

Before ISIS came, these were normal boys who

went to school, watched television, played with their friends, respected their parents and saw a future for themselves studying, and then a good job and of course a fast car. The war in Syria had changed their lives even before ISIS captured their city, but it was the domination of this radical group which altered their view of the world. ISIS brought them back to what it called the ideal time, fourteen centuries ago, the time of the Prophet Mohammed.

And just as important: they were taught to believe that the end of times was near, and that their real goal in life must be reaching paradise in the next life.

≈ ≈ ≈

Indoctrination is the problem of the near future, and not only for the boys. The photos circulated by ISIS show that girls at school and during training are being just as brainwashed as the boys. Even though their role in the caliphate is different, there is no room for them for personal ambitions: they are the mothers of the future. These young people are the property of ISIS, and they are ticking time bombs within their society.

After the liberation, mid-2017, of the last cities ISIS occupied in Iraq, hundreds of young boys ended up in prison, mostly Arab but also some Yazidi. Some of them had been involved in the fighting, others had just been trained an indoctrinated. International organizations trained social workers on de-radicalization programs in the prisons, but putting these boys together in closed departments might ruin the effect of those programs. ISIS was born in prison, and might return from prison too, as many radicalization experts have pointed out.

Local boys who went to ISIS schools were mostly taken back into the new school programs after the liberation, where teachers tried to erase the bad influences of the radicals, as they told me when I visited schools in Mosul. Most children I saw, both boys and girls, were traumatized because of the violence ISIS had inflicted on the society, but also because of the heavy bombardments by the coalition forces and their flight out of the burning city.

≈≈≈

The occupation by ISIS has also left heavy scars on the Yazidi region of Sinjar. Some will be permanent. When I visited the region in early 2015, not long after the partial liberation, I noticed especially the destruction and the doors that were open everywhere, because ISIS fighters had looted the homes. The small electrical plant had been largely dismantled; all useful materials were taken to Syria. But what struck me more than anything else was the fact that a few hundred people had dared to return. That number barely increased in the following months, with the exception of a single farmer working on his land and harvesting his crops. When I wanted to use the toilet, it turned out that in the house where people were living there was no water or electricity. This is not very inviting to return to.

And yet that is not what still is preventing the Yazidis from returning after ISIS was kicked out completely. It is the threat from Arabic villagers who have returned. Yazidis view the Arabic villages, which are spread throughout the entire Sinjar region, as a grave danger. 'We can no longer trust any Arabs,' a local Yazidi militia leader told me. 'They helped Daesh, killed Yazidis and took our women and girls. We can never live with them again.' There are even claims that a small portion of the Yazidi women were imprisoned by them; that Arab neighbors worked alongside ISIS and then took a woman as a slave themselves.

≈≈≈

After the liberation was declared against ISIS, in July 2017, the situation in Sinjar became over more complicated, as different military groups divided the area between them: the militias of the Shiite Hashed al-Shabi (from Baghdad), Kurds and Yezidis who joined the fighters of the (Turkish-Kurdish) PKK, and peshmerga troops from Iraqi Kurdistan. At the same time, hardly any explosives were cleared and rebuilding has not started.

In a recaptured Sinjar, eventually the demographics will change. Everyone I speak to, expects that many Yazidis will eventually have to return home. Their possessions are there, their land, their culture and their history. But with the Arabs they no longer want to live, so a solution must be found.

To prepare for the return, a few local NGO's, including the Emma Organization for Humanitarian Development, for which Bayan Rasul is active, and the Seed Foundation of Sherri Kraham, with aid from the Netherlands worked on a development plan for Sinjar. It is a kind of road map for the Kurdish and Iraqi governments, with suggestions for economic and agricultural development, education, administration and even the establishment of a special museum about this genocide, as the Kurds call the tragedy.

Strikingly, the very central matter of the distrust between the Yazidis and their Arab neighbors is not mentioned. 'That is something we must work on,' Tanya Gilly from the Seed Foundation agrees. 'But first we must ensure that there is safety. The army must remove weapons and explosives. Then people must know what can be expected: can they return? Through this, the trust will grow.' And the Yazidis must know who will protect them. In this, the Kurdish government is an important player, Gilly says. 'If people see that it is safe, the other steps which we have proposed will follow naturally.'

≈ ≈ ≈

The advance of ISIS also has had other consequences. In Iraqi Kurdistan, which had in the fight against ISIS lost almost 2,000 soldiers, many people distanced themselves from the Islamic faith. This was evident by the empty mosques: the number of visitors dropped by 40 percent, according to the Kurdish Ministry of Religion.

That was partly due to the fact that parents kept their teen-aged sons at home, out of fear that they would feel drawn towards Salafism and then travel to the frontline. Others disagreed with the ideas of their imam. Despite the fact that of the around 3,000 imams in Kurdistan only 74 are listed as being Salafist, many imams still maintain extremely conservative ideas. In the summer of 2018, the Kurdish security police still arrested one who had ties to ISIS, after he set three young Kurdish teenagers onto a deadly raid of the Governors Building in central Erbil.

A Kurdish girlfriend voiced her repulsion by posting on Facebook that she would not celebrate a single Islamic feast, 'until the liberation of our girls and the country out of the filthy hands of the Islamists.' Others turned completely away from

Islam and converted to Zoroastrianism, also known under the name of the founder Zarathustra with whom it originated in the region some 2,500 years ago. This monotheistic faith, which is said to already have thousands of followers, was officially registered by the Kurdish Ministry of Religion in July of 2015, allowing it to start (re)building their temples. When I asked one of the followers whether he was concerned about the wrath of ISIS, he answered that the time for secrecy is over. 'We have made our decision and that could have consequences. The only thing that ISIS can do, is to murder. We are not afraid; its religion is backward.'

≈≈≈

In the story about ISIS, women are both victims and accomplices – or they are on the side lines helping to gather up the debris. But could women also help in bringing a halt to ISIS, and damming up the growth of radicalism? Do they have a choice, as a mother and wife, to not join in the radicalization around them and therefore become an accomplice? Can they possibly prevent their sons and husbands from allowing themselves to be swept away by it all?

Carla Koppell, a gender specialist from the United States Agency for International Development (USAID) says in an opinion piece in Foreign Policy, that the position of women is underestimated. 'Around the world, women have critical traditional and contemporary roles to leverage in blunting the impact of extremism. Women often have influence within the family, giving them enormous potential to stem recruitment and radicalization.'

Moreover, women and girls who remain behind in conflict areas to care for the children and other family members, often have valuable information and insights. They can serve as a timely warning for conflicts and potential violence, she says. And for the same reasons they can help with the de-radicalization and reintegration into society of former members of extremist groups.

'Sisters against violent extremism' is an appealing example; an initiative of an Austrian NGO to establish schools along the border between Afghanistan and Tadzhikistan for mothers, and to teach them how they can fight the radicalization of their sons. Over a 150 mothers have been trained there already. Furthermore, local meetings have been organized with the police, to point out to the policemen in which way the women can best exert influence.

Gender advisor Idah Muema of the United Nations Mission in Iraq (UNAMI), who I met in Erbil at a seminar about sexual violence in conflict situations, also believes women can help to fight terrorism, violence and radicalization. 'Radicalization cannot be fought solely with military actions. We need soft tools,' she says. This means 'working with unsatisfied communities, working with youths, the promotion of tolerance and social inclusion.'

Muema is excited that the Iraqi government has decided to name August 15th as a national day against sexual violence in conflict situations. This means Baghdad at least recognizes the problem. She points out that the UN Security Council has accepted four resolutions since 2008 to prevent and fight conflict-related sexual violence. To involve women in the prevention, they must also be mobilized to maintain the peace and security and in peace building.

How important it is to inform women about the ways in which they can shield their children from radicalization, is clear from the story of the Turks-Kurdish Hatice in the Turkish city of Adiyaman, whose son was recruited by ISIS. He was involved in an attack during a Kurdish demonstration in Diyarbakır in the summer of 2015. She told Public Radio International (PRI) why she suspected that things were going wrong with him. Orhan had grown a beard, prayed five times a day and had new friends. She spoke to him about this: had he been in contact with radical groups from Syria? He adamantly denied this.

Hatice even tried to get her son out of the country, to her sister in France. But he refused; he did not know the language, so what would he do there? He tried to reassure his mother: 'I only want to learn more about Islam.' She thinks that he had been put under great pressure to carry out the attack. Once he landed in prison, he was overflowing with remorse.

Her demand was to deal with the recruiters first, who in their town Adiyaman have recruited at least thirty boys. The mayor of Adiyaman, Hüsrev Kutlu repeated that plea. The bomb makers and those carrying out the attacks were not the real guilty ones, he believed. 'No one had even done something like this if they had not been brainwashed.'

The recruiters are not always easy to find; many of them work after all through the internet, and out of the caliphate. In the West, recruiters who are caught are then arrested, just like youths who want to travel to Syria. They are charged with belonging to a terrorist organization, but are not always convicted.

In Iraq, UNAMI works with various partners on a system to record the many laws being broken by ISIS supporters. These vary from theft, kidnapping, murder, violation of human rights to sexual violence. A list of offenders is also being compiled against whom the UN must undertake measures, with at the very top Abu Bakr al-Baghdadi. In June 2016, the United Nations state that ISIS is committing genocide against the Yazidis in Syria and Iraq to destroy the religious community through killings, sexual slavery and other crimes. This decision could aid the prosecution of ISIS perpetrators.

Bringing sexual violence offenders in conflict

situations to justice is a 'challenge,' as Muema puts it. 'You can hold the leaders of militias and armed groups responsible for the sexual violence taking place under their command. But over the whole world, we have only been able to prosecute a few.'

But as Iraq and the Kurdistan Region started to convict the around 13.000 men they hold for ISIS crimes, none of them were actually charged and tried because of sexual violence or their part of the Yazidi genocide. The verdicts in Baghdad were relatively simple: those with blood on their hands were convicted to death, those who assisted or only were trained to prison.

≈≈≈

The big fish with ISIS, after 2017 are based in obscure areas in Iraq and Syria. That is where the strategies are designed; where the survival of the caliphate is planned. How can you ever prosecute those responsible? I talked about this with a Kurdish human rights lawyer, Govand Baban, who has defended activists for years, and also does censorship cases. In the battle against ISIS, he did not reach for the weapon of the law, but instead for a Kalashnikov; he joined the Kurdish fighters, the Peshmerga. 'For ISIS supporters there are no human rights, because they have come to destroy us,' he announces.

The slightly balding man in his fifties surprises

me in his office at the UKH, the English-language university in Erbil, by reaching for the tissues. As he talks about how threatened he felt when in August of 2014 ISIS came at a distance of no more than 30 kilometers from our city of Erbil, he is months later still moved to tears. 'We are not fighting a country,' he says when he has calmed down. 'And what are the rules; which UN agreement applies? We do not know.'

Whoever was captured on the battlefield, stayed with the security service of the Kurdish Peshmerga to be interrogated. For a long time, little was known about the fate of ISIS prisoners of war. Because the Kurds had not reported them as being prisoners of war, which is against international rules, the International Red Cross could not visit them. The same applied to those held by the Iraqi authorities, but changed when in 2017 the juridical system started to process them. But it was known that the ISIS fighters came from everywhere: Egypt, Sudan, Tunisia, Russia and several European countries. They are mostly charged with membership of a terrorist organization.

Initially, they were all men, just like the alleged organizers of bombings in the Kurdish capital and the 'sleeper cells' who have been arrested in Kurdistan. Women were amongst the infiltrators arrested: Saadjihah, a niece of ISIS leader Baghdadi, Baban tells me, and the sister mentioned in chapter six of one of his wives who wanted to carry out suicide attacks in Kurdistan. Baban expected that she will never be sentenced.

And then there is Umm Sayyaf, who, as described in chapter 5, was arrested during an American raid in Syria where her husband, the high-ranking ISIS official Abu Sayyaf was killed. She must stand trial in Kurdistan. The Americans handed her over to the Kurds with this order. It would have been more logical to burden Baghdad with this, given the fact that she is an Iraqi, and not Kurdish. Moreover, the Kurds have no experience with sentencing terror suspects of this level. What played a role for the Americans, is that the victims of Umm Sayyaf were predominantly Kurdish: the dozens of Yazidi women she delivered as slaves to the ISIS fighters.

≈≈≈

Other women involved with ISIS, among them foreigners, were arrested after they fled the last ISIS strongholds in 2017. They have since all been handed over to Baghdad, that has been trying the women the same way as the men: even dozens of foreign women were given the death penalty. Hundreds of the foreign women who had been recruited by ISIS, by mid-2018 were stuck in prison camps in Syria. The Kurdish authorities there were begging their countries to take them back – with their children born in the caliphate – but most countries are not eager to do so.

For the escaped Yazidi women, no court case can bring back their murdered husbands, brothers and sons. Nor their relatively carefree lives, their honor or their future. No wonder that they, when I ask about it, wish the worst of the worst for their former captors. 'If it was up to me, I would kill them all,' Hanna says, who became pregnant from a Russian. 'Treat them like they treated us Yazidis. Kill them all,' Khanu says too, who managed to escape with her two sons. 'Burn them,' Khansi demands, who hid her daughter in cupboards to keep her out of the hands of ISIS fighters.

≈ ≈ ≈

The last words of this chapter I happily give to Vian Dakhil, the Yazidi member of the Iraqi parliament who gained international fame with her emotional plea to save the Yazidis, when ISIS was kidnapping and murdering them in August of 2014. She too was involved with the question of prosecution and working on changes to Iraqi criminal law to better convict accomplices. 'Everyone who has attacked the Yazidis, or helped in doing this, must be prosecuted,' she said to me in 2015. 'I am receiving much support for this in the parliament.'

Twice she mentioned that the attitude of the wives

of men who had joined ISIS baffled her. 'I do not understand them; how they can stay with a man who rapes a young girl. If that Yazidi girl escapes, he will rape his daughter, or his sister – because he is sick.'

We were silent together while we processed this reality: what ISIS wreaks is virtually impossible to restore and it will have consequences for the lives of women in this region for many years to come.

Just like many others in my surroundings, I have great admiration for Vian Dakhil. I know her from the time that she was the assistant to the then chairman of the Kurdish parliament, Kamal Kirkuki. She arranged a meeting with him that eventually led to a training for Kurdish parliamentarians.

On a hot summer evening, she received me in her home in Erbil, which I could not miss thanks to the guards in the street. Her secretary brought a bottle of cold water and a small cup of strong coffee, while the air conditioner had difficulty in driving out the heat of the day from the large reception area. It differed little with those of other Kurdish dignitaries: chairs, couches, curtains and lamps in Baroque style, and many small side tables. Dark red and brown tints were predominant.

She told me how her life had changed, since the organized robbery and murder of 'her people', how it dominated her life, and she lost her private life. 'It is not easy. People expect that I can solve their problems. Yesterday I did not sleep, because one of our girls in the camps has a serious problem and I was fretting about what I could do for her.'

She affirmed that she has in fact become an ambassador for the Yazidis. And then, soberly said this new position also brings about that people listen to her. 'Every time I am on the television, I say to the Yazidis that each of the returning women is one of us, that we must accept them because they are victims. Sometimes Baba Sheik asks me: "Vian, can you tell the families this, because these people now love you."' It is a heavy responsibility, she admitted. 'I do everything I can, even though I know that it is never enough.'

Dakhil was the only Yazidi among the 328 members of the Iraqi parliament in Bagdad. That was lonely. 'It is not easy when you are a woman, Yazidi and Kurdish, do not wear a headscarf, and then also continually lead the conversation...' For example, on the day she gave her famous speech in parliament, she was attacked by parliament members who were angry that she was accusing Arabs of atrocities against the Yazidis. 'Some hate me. My god, yes, during that speech... A Sunni parliament member was angry with me. And later on, I was attacked in the restaurant of the parliament by a Shiite woman in an abaya.'

She had not expected this from another woman. We shared our disappointment over the lack of international women's solidarity with the Yazidi women. 'International women's organizations are silent! Nothing comes from the people who are always talking about human rights. Not even here in Kurdistan. Perhaps that would have been different if the victims had not been Yazidis. Only from Kak Masoud [the former President Barzani, JN] do I hear that he cries every time I talk about the Yazidi girls.'

I know that this is not entirely true, because I know women's organizations in Kurdistan who have collected clothing and sewn white robes for fleeing Yazidi women; I have girlfriends who organized fundraisers, while women like Sherri Kraham undertake initiatives to bring aid. But Dakhil was right about the protests against ISIS and actions to liberate the women: nearly all derived only from the Yazidis themselves.

The liberations were undertaken by Yazidis. A Yazidi businessman who lived in Kurdistan nearly had a full-time job in doing this: he had managed to get some three hundred Yazidis out of the hands of ISIS by paying amounts varying from 6,000 and 35,000 dollars (5,130 to more than 29,925 Euros) per person. In total I meet three of these Yazidi men, all used their contacts, set up a network and worked tirelessly for four years to get the daughters of their community out.

Dakhil pulled herself together to show her admiration for the help the Kurds had given, and to emphasize how important it was that the Kurdish government supported families financially who bought back their women. But she accused the Iraqi government of talking about the liberation of the Arab territories, but at the same time placing Sinjar at the end of the list. 'Whenever I speak to the governments in Bagdad and Erbil, or international governments, I repeat that the time has come to do something for our missing. I beg the Iraqi government for help; with funding, or a military liberation action. That must still be possible. But it seems like Bagdad does not feel responsible for us. They do nothing to liberate our people.'

≈ ≈ ≈

Especially when she was abroad, she realized just how important her speech has been. 'It has touched the world. Before then, no one knew anything about the Yazidis. When I went to Washington and the European Parliament, people told me that they had never heard about the Yazidis before.' She called for the realization of a peacekeeping force, to protect Sinjar once the region is liberated. Such a UN force would especially have to guard the border with Syria to prevent ISIS from returning. It never materialized. Her standpoint was contradictory, as she wanted the presence of these blue helmets so the Yazidis would feel more safe. But these were mainly concerned about the Arab population of Sinjar. Dakhil admitted: 'What happened to us was not only done by ISIS supporters from outside Sinjar, but especially by Iraqis, our neighbors. The Arab villagers helped ISIS. How can we return and live together with these people again? We have lost our trust.'

It is an important obstacle for the goal that the Yazidis eventually return home, but by far not the only one. Many were still in a state of shock, Dakhil said. 'They are only thinking of surviving, what they have to eat, that there is no water... In a few years, when our people are back in Sinjar, then we will have to deal with many psychological problems. Especially amongst the women who are unable to understand what has happened, and are unable to accept it.'

That the majority of the returning women have been accepted back into the community without too many problems, is mainly thanks to the statement of the Baba Sheik, she said. 'All Yazidis listen to him, I am happy to say.' But not only is the spiritual leader old and no one knows if his successor will enjoy the same obedience, it is also impossible to predict the actions of people in the future, once they have returned to their old surroundings, and how they will view the former sex slaves.

Due to this uncertainty, but also due to the hopelessness of the existence in a tent in a camp for years on end, many Yazidis want to leave Iraq. 'It is a big problem. They want a new life in Europe. I do not like it, but I cannot forbid it. I have nothing to offer them. No work, no income, no clear future...' Dakhil sighed. It would also be a loss for the region if so many people would leave, she then said. 'Kurdistan is so special, thanks to all the various religious communities. And do not forget that it is our country; we are the original Kurds.'

In order to offer people a realistic choice, Dakhil was working hard on plans for 'after ISIS'. Sinjar has been completely plundered, and rebuilding does not only apply for buildings and infrastructure, but also for pride and unity. 'We must teach people that it is important to return, because it is our land. We have to protect this, against ISIS and all others.' Solemnly she said: 'What has happened, has happened. Now we must continue with a new life.'

Epilogue

The first time I walk around in Mosul after the liberation, it feels very unreal. It's early 2017, and only the Eastern half of the city has been freed of ISIS. The scars of the liberation are everywhere: ruins, damaged houses, churches and mosques, broken roads and lamp posts. But also, the scars of three years of ISIS rule, even though the graffiti for the Islamic State has already mostly been removed: the dirt, the squalor, the dereliction.

And the less visible scars. What these years have done to women is far more difficult to assess, although the first thing that strikes me is the way they dress now: there is hardly any black dress or scarf around anymore, and the despised niqaab has almost completely left the scene.

I decide to interview women about their experiences and combine those into another book:

Women survive ISIS. Because I wonder, if it is possible that something so negative, can also have positive results? Kurdish sociologist Chnar Abdullah told me in an interview that with the tragedy of the Yazidis – the kidnapping and murdering of thousands by ISIS – she was still able to see a silver lining.

Abdullah concluded that the closed society of the Yazidis is opening up under the pressure of what has happened to their women. What normally would be a long process, now happens at a greatly accelerated pace. 'The war has sad consequences, but we will also see positivity in the future. The society will no longer be the same. It will be more open, the level of education will be raised, the role of women will increase, and the power of the religion will diminish.'

The changes actually began with the return of the raped women. Thanks to a decision by the religious leadership of the Yazidis, they were cleansed of any blame. Abdullah viewed this as being defining for the reaction of the group and the changes it is experiencing. 'Previously, a girl who had fallen in love with someone from another faith, would have been murdered! But now, they view the women as victims and try not to kill them. That means that the society is trying to break with old values.'

The sociologist saw that women who had returned, were going through an emancipation process. Like for example Nadia Murad, a young

Yazidi woman who publicly and repeatedly told the story of her kidnapping, repeated sale and rape, and by doing so gained global attention for the fate of the Yazidis under the control of ISIS. 'If these crimes had not been committed, we would have perhaps never even heard her name. Now we not only know her, but many other Nadias as well.'

≈≈≈

This transition will not be an easy one, Abdullah warned. 'There will be problems. Conflicts between young and old, women and men. But the clock cannot be turned back anymore.' At the same time, she emphasized that the negative effect of what happened cannot be denied. 'Not only will this generation be traumatized, but also the next. What happened under ISIS will haunt these women for the rest of their lives.'

But from the adagio 'what doesn't kill you makes you stronger,' the horrific experiences under ISIS could in the long term also lead to growth and development.

ISIS treated all women badly, but with the Yazidis that was a superlative degree. Will only struggling up from the deepest depths of humiliation, lead to change? Or will the women of Mosul and other occupied cities come out stronger after the horrors they have survived? And what happens to the women on the other side: those who joined ISIS, or married the fighters and supporters?

I visit them in 2017, in the Shahama camp, just outside of Tikrit, where some 350 ISIS families are locked up. I am the first journalist to speak to them. The families – especially women and children, but also some married couples and older men – are totally cut off from the outside world, with no visitors and no access even to phones.

'They are afraid that we will pass along information to Daesh,' Samara Musa (35) tells me, who lives in a tent in the camp, along with nine children. Since she is not allowed to have a phone, for some time now she has not received any news about her husband. He was arrested by the Iraqi army, 'because his brother was with Daesh,' she says. This brother is now with ISIS in Syria. 'We had arguments with him. We were not part of Daesh, and we also received nothing from them.'

This is what the majority of the women tell me: a son, husband, father or brother joined, the families opposed this but were left powerless and are now being punished. The detained family members feel they are victims, although most do admit to initially being happy with the arrival of ISIS. However, they say they had realized within months what the group was really about.

I sense this feeling of being a victim in all of my interviews. 'I don't even have the money to buy a kilo of tomatoes,' Saheya Ibrahim complains. This woman is in the camp with her husband. They tried in vain to stop their son, when he wanted to join ISIS, just as his uncle – her brother. Where they are now, they do not know. Nor do they know the whereabouts of her second son, who was arrested by the army due to his family's ties with ISIS.

≈ ≈ ≈

In the months following my visit, this becomes a major issue: many families do not know if their sons or husbands are still alive, or in jail. And as the Iraqi justice system gathers steam, many of them are sentenced to death, or at the best to long prison sentences.

Shahama, which opened in January 2017, is not the only camp for ISIS family members in Iraq. Still others flee along with the refugees from Tikrit, Fallujah and Mosul onto the camps for displaced persons – some go underground, but more often they are known to the authorities and shunned by other refugees, who have lost family members due to the ISIS regime. Yet it is hard to find women who will admit they made a conscious choice for ISIS.

When I ask the women in Shahama how they feel about the group, they are united in their condemnation of it. 'They are infidels,' according to

Iman Hazem Ismael (47), a thin widow who saw two of her five sons join ISIS. They were seventeen and twenty then, and later killed during gunfire by the Iraqi army.

The management of the camp reports that Hazem actively worked with the ISIS regime by conducting body searches on women. She is aware of the accusation, she says impassively, but it is all nonsense.

She claims to have asked her sons to leave ISIS. And was herself even beaten by ISIS, and threatened with the execution of her other sons, after she had attempted to escape.

I would like to believe her, but then she tells me that the baby sleeping next to her in the stifling hot tent is her daughter's, who was married to an emir (a leader) of ISIS. She has fled to Syria with her husband and father-in-law. So next to her two sons who were fighting with ISIS, she also has a daughter who was involved with them. And as family of the fighters, ISIS sent them all to Mosul. When the Iraqi army liberated East-Mosul, ISIS put them on boats across the Tigris to the still occupied western part of the city, where they would eventually surrender to the army. Just how involved are you then?

If she is a supporter of ISIS, then she is not prepared to admit to this fact. And the only thing I can ascertain from the process that led to her making this choice is that she, like many other Sunnis, initially viewed ISIS as the salvation from the discriminating regime of the Shiite majority that came into power in Iraq after the fall of Saddam Hussein.

Most of the women complain about the hopelessness of the situation; where can they go? 'I don't think that we will be able to live with the people,' Hazem concludes when asked about her future. 'My oldest son has done too much to too many people. He made a huge mistake.'

Hazem would like to live somewhere, where no one knows her. 'I just want to feel like an Iraqi once more. Here they only call us Daesh families. We have to be rid of that.'

In Mosul, I am told that there is fear for the supporters of ISIS who have gone into hiding, and that no one knows whether their families can be trusted, because they might still be actively working for the group. After talking to Hazem, I can fully understand this doubt: is she a victim or a culprit, or both?

~ ~ ~

Another element to this saga becomes clear, when I interview a Turkman family in a refugee camp outside Mosul. Here are the families that were the last to leave the city – and therefore probably were involved with ISIS. When I talk to the mother – who is there without husband or sons – I notice the ages of the children are too close together, and some are too young for a woman of her age. Soon after, I am confronted with the fact that Yazidi women and children are being found with families like these. They were kidnapped from Sinjar, and now are often too scared and indoctrinated to come forward. I conclude that at least one of the boys I saw that day, could be Yazidi. A difficult search is started to reunite these Yazidis with their remaining family members in Kurdistan.

It is also important, because the longer they remain in the clutches of ISIS, the more they are changed. Yazidi doctor and volunteer Mirza Dinnayi tells me, that women who were freed after three years or more, were convinced that all of the Yazidis had been exterminated, and therefore there was not a single reason left for them anymore to want to attempt an escape. Moreover, many women are now so psychologically damaged by the brutality they have been subjected to for years, that they will never be able to have a normal life without receiving professional help.

As for the ISIS wives, they all share the stigma that will control their remaining lives, including all those who had a jihad al-nikah or were forced into a marriage. Many women will go underground, or move to a place where no one knows them, leaving their family and friends behind. At least, if they have the financial means to do so. Perhaps they will survive by denying that they made a conscious choice, and claiming that they are victims because their husbands were lured into ISIS. For many civilians, I find, that is also how they prefer to see the situation.

≈ ≈ ≈

The women who survived the occupation, will also bear the scars. Not only due to ISIS, but also from the liberation. The violence that partly was directed towards them, resulted in many traumas. Like for students in East-Mosul, who complained to me about having problems concentrating. Nora (22) recounted how ISIS evicted her and her family from their home, when the Iraqi army was getting closer. 'We had to walk to another occupied neighborhood – in the dark, to prevent the airplanes from seeing us. With only the clothes on our backs we lived with some family for forty-one days.' Fatma (19) was also forced to leave. 'We had to crawl through the holes they had made in the walls between our houses. Three days later, our house was liberated. We found bombs and military items there, because Daesh had used it.'

The memories haunt them, and the young women became very emotional when telling their stories. They told me about an uncle, who ISIS arrested when he tried to escape. About snipers in their neighborhood. And Ayat's eyes filled with tears, when she talked about her sister being killed by mortars ISIS fired into their neighborhood during the battle with the Iraqi army.

After three years of ISIS occupation, all citizens of Mosul must once again learn to trust, or perhaps even learn to live with distrust. Women must reclaim their position in society, get back to work, and regain respect. And at the same time, they must see to it that their children do not suffer any lasting damage, do not become radicalized or perhaps turn their backs on the Islamic faith all together – like is happening in Iraq, out of repulsion against ISIS' religious legacy.

I hope that the dismissal of ISIS' standards leads to more freedom than before, and that the closed society in a city like Mosul will open more swiftly than normally would be expected, such as is evident with the Yazidis. But as yet, there are not sufficient signs that this hope will become reality.

What doesn't kill you makes you stronger. Is that also true for the women of Mosul? Perhaps for some. Let me share the words of some students, who managed to see the positive effects in all of this. Nora said to me that she has learned to be more patient. Amina believed that she has grown through all the misery. And Muntar concluded: 'We were sitting in the middle of death, and we survived.'

WORD OF THANKS

This book could not have been realized without the many Yazidi women and girls who were willing to share their gruesome stories with me. I am in indebted to them, and I have great admiration for the women who have survived and are trying to pick up their lives again.

I am also thankful to the women, and some men, who took the risk of giving me information from inside Mosul.

I thank Sharaf and Hazim, young men who took on the difficult task of translating the testimonies of the Yazidi women for me, and Areen and Sozy for whom that was easier as a woman, but certainly no less burdening. Thanks too for Halgurd, who did his best to translate explanations about the Quran into understandable English.

Special thanks go to my good friend and colleague Khidher Domle, for his trust and contributions, and also for continually pointing out new sources to me.

I want to thank Amina and Jameel, who both lead an organization which has taken on realizing the registration of the Yazidis, recording their stories and in helping them with their return to society. And Nasreen, who seems to know nearly all of the escaped Yazidis and helped me and my translators Hazim and Sharaf to find the right people to talk to.

Also my chauffeur Hoger I want to thank, for the many long drives in the Duhok region, for his care and concern about my safety and his patience when he had to wait for hours until my interviews were finished. And I also thank my friends Akram Jibouri, Shivan Fazel, Kurda Daloye and Deborah Morgan-Jones, who were always willing to listen when I needed to share the gruesome facts from the interviews.

Many thanks too, for my fellow readers Nynke La Porte, Els Horst and Pamela Williams, who stood by me with critical comments, suggestions and encouragement.

And also thanks for my many colleagues who just like me also report about this region, with some being able to make articles for which a freelancer like myself had neither the time nor the means. From their stories I have made grateful use to fill eventual gaps. I have made every effort to name them all in the list of sources.

And finally thanks for my Dutch publisher Jurgen Maas, who gave me the opportunity to write and publish this book. He gave me a great deal of freedom and stimulated me by his trust in me to continue, even when the current events engulfed me once again.

I updated this book in July 2018, added an epilogue and changed the title and the cover, which had been found not fitting for some of the markets. And I want it to reach as many people as possible, as the story of what ISIS did to women should be known all over the world, to prevent horrors like these from repeating themselves.

To pick up the story of the women of ISIS, I wrote a long-read called *Women Survive ISIS*, which is available as an e-book in the Amazon-stores.

If you enjoyed this book, I am sure you will also love to read my suspenseful novel *The Good Terrorist*, where I used many elements from the ISIS-story. Read a segment of the book on the next pages.

Also, it would be great to keep you updated about my activities as a writer. Sign up for my newsletter, and receive a short novella for free, by going to my website: https://juditneurinkauthor.com/free-book-for-you/

Judit Neurink, Athens, July 2018/August 2023

LIST OF SOURCES

Abouzeid, Rania, 'Out of Sight', The New Yorker, October 5, 2015, www.thenewyorker.com/magazine/2015/10/05/out-of-sight-letter-from-baghdad-rania-abouzeid.

Ahmad, Rozh, 'Q&A with former Islamic State member', Your Middle East, September 28, 2014, www.yourmiddleeast.com/culture/exclusive-qa-with-former-islamic-state-member_26696.

Al-Muhajirah, 'Umm Sumayyah, Slave-Girls or Prostitutes', Dabiq nr. 9, May 2015, via http://media.clarionproject.org/files/islamic-state/isis-isil-islamic-state-magazine-issue%2B9-they-plot-and-allah-plots-sex-slavery.pdf

Blair, Leonardo, 'Inside ISIS: Fighters Promised "74 Eternal Virgins in Heaven" While Christian Women Raped as Husbands Beheaded, Says Ex-Member', The Christian Post, September 19, 2014, www.christianpost.com/news/inside-isis-fighters-promised-72-eternal-virgins-in-heaven-while-christian-women-raped-as-husbands-beheaded-says-ex-member-126710/.

Bolwijn, Marjol, 'Women in war are just as cruel as men', de Volkskrant, April 1, 2015, www.volkskrant.nl/wetenschap/vrouwen-zijn-net-zo-wreed-als-mannen-tijdens-oorlog~a3941813/.

Callimachi, Rukmini, 'ISIS and the Lonely Young American, Flirting With the Islamic State', The New York Times, June 27, 2015, http://mibile.nytimes.com/2015/06/28/world/americas/isis-online-recruiting-american.html?referrer=&_r=0.

Callimachi, Rukmini, 'ISIS Enshrines a Theology of Rape', The New York Times, August 13, 2015, http://www.nytimes.com/2015/08/14/world/middleeast/isis-enshrines-a-theology-of-rape.html

Creswell, Robyn and Haykel, Berhard, 'Battle lines: Want to understand jihadis? Read their poetry', The New Yorker, June 8, 2015, www.newyorker.com/magazine/2015/06-08/battle-lines-jihad-creswell-and-haykel.

Dabiq, internet magazine of ISIS, www.clarionproject.org/news/islamic-state-isis-isil-propoganda-magazine-dabiq.

Domle. Khidher, The Black Death. Duhok: in own control. 2015.

El Deeb, Sarah, 'For an IS fighter, a paid honeymoon in the caliphate's heart', Associated

Press, May 26, 2015, http://bigstory.ap.org.urn:publicid:ap.org:7f320b20cd5d46789aa413be19039401.

Erelle, Anne, In the Skin of a Jihadist: Inside Islamic State's Recruitment Networks. New York: HarperCollins, 2015.

Fantz, Ashley and Shubert, Atika, 'From Scottish teen to ISIS bride and recruiter: the Aqsa Mahmood story/2015/02/23/world/Scottish-teen-isis-recruiter/.

George, Susannah, 'Yazidi Women Welcomed Back to the Faith', UNHCR TRACKS, June 2015, http://tracks.unhcr.org/2015/06/yazidi-women-welcomed-back-to-the-faith/.

Glanfield, Emma. 'British jihadi bride who fled to Syria has written guide on how to be a war widow, sparking rumours her husband has been killed', Mail Online, January 25, 2015, www.daily.mail.co.uk/news/article-2925844/British-jihadi-bride-fled-Syria-written-guide-war-widow-sparking-rumours-husband-killed.html.

Gillman, Ollie, 'Dutch jihadist girl, 19, rescued from Syria by her mother lived a happy life cooking for Islamists and doing "girl stuff", says her terrorist ex-husband', Mail Online, November 23, 2014, www.dailymail.co.uk/news/article-2846059/Dutch-jihadist-girl-rescued-Syria-mother-lived-happy-life-cooking-Islamists-doing-girl-stuff-says-terrorist-ex-husband.html.

'Hijrah to the Islamic State, What to pack, who to contact, where to go', Prequel e-book Islamic State, 2015. https://thejihadiproject.files.wordpress.com/2015/05/hijrah-to-the-islamic-state.pdf.

Hilsum, Lindsey, 'Life under Islamic State: the devotion of some young Syrians, Channel 4, June 17, 2015, http://blogs.channel4.com/lindsey-hilsum-on-international-affairs/life-islamic-state-devotion-young-syrians/5340#sthash.XOPXqiYd.dpuf

Hubbard, Ben, 'Offering Services. ISIS Digs In Deeper in Seized Territories', The New York Times, June 16, 2015,www.nytimes.com/2015/06/17/world/middleeast/offering-services-isis-enscones-itself-in-seized-territories.html.

Karam, Zeina, 'Inside Islamic State group's rule: Creating a nation of fear', AP The Big Story, June 17, 2015, http://bigstory.ap.org/urn:publicid:ap:org:107f1977ef8241d9865649d03ac5816f.

Katz, Rita, 'From Teenage Colorado Girls to Islamic State Recruits: A Cade Study in Radicalization Via Social Media', Intelligence Group, November 11, 2014, http://news.siteintelgroup.com/blog/index.php/entry/309-from-teenage-colorado-girls-to-islamic-state-recruits-a-case-study-in-radicalization-via-social-media.

Koppell, Carla, 'To Fight Extremism, the World Needs to Learn How to Talk to Women, Foreign Policy, August 12, 2015, https://foreignpolicy.com/2015.08/12/to-fight-extremism-the-world-needs-to-learn-how-to-talk-to-women-boko-haram-isis/.

Mosendz, Polly, 'How a Teenager Travels to Join the Islamic State', Newsweek, March 3, 2015, www.newsweek.com/how-teenager-travels-join islamic-state-310710.

Mosul Eye, https://www.facebook.com/pages/Mosul-Eye/55251484487022.

Mustafah, Ruwayda, 'Family shuns Yezidi teen impregnated by ISIS, Rudaw, May 27, 2015, http://rudaw.net/english/blog-27052015112437.

Naylor, Seán D, 'Exclusive: American Hostage Passed on Chance to Escape', Foreign Policy, May 22, 2015, http://foreignpolicy/2015/05/22/exclusive-american-hostage-passed-on-chance-to-escapre-kayla-mueller-abu-sayyaf-delta-force/.

Neurink, Judit, De oorlog van ISIS. Schoorl: Uitgeverij Conserve, 2015. The War of ISIS, Amazon, 2016

Neurink, Judit, Misleide martelaren. Contact, 2005.

O'Flynn, Eliano, 'Huge numbers of Muslims are returning to ISIS because they want SEX, claims former Islamist, who says many resent the freedoms

Western youths have', Mail Online, June 16, 2015, www.dailymail.co.uk/news.article.-3126987/Huge-numbers-Muslims-turning-ISIS-want-SEX-reveals-former-Islamist-says-resent-freedoms-Western-youths-have.html.

Olivesi, Marine, 'ISIS recruited my son 'because he's Kurdish', PRI's The World, August 12, 2015, www.pri.org/stories/2015-08-12/isis-recruited-my-son-because-hes-kurdish.

Olmer, Bart '"Geredde" jihadi onveranderd radicaal, Sterlina P. opnieuw islamitisch getrouwd en volledig gesluierd', De Telegraaf, March 31, 2015, www.telegraaf.nl/binnenland.23868359/___Geredde__ _jihadibruid_radicaal___.html?utm_source=t.co&utm_medium=referral&utm_campaign=twitter.

'One Year Since Mosul', TSG Intel brief The Soufan Group, June 10, 2015, http://soufangroup.com/tsg-intelbrief-one-year-since-mosul/.

Paraszcuk, Joanna, 'Ghazala's Story: Whether We Live Or Die, The Important Thing Is To Escape', Radio Free Europe/Radio Liberty, June 19, 2015, www.rferl.org/content/islamic-state-yazidi-woman-s-ordeal/27081860.html.

Pellegrini-Bettoli, Gaja, 'Assyrian Christian woman shares story of captivity by Islamic State', Al-Monitor, July 30, 2015, www.al-monitor.com/pulse/originals/2015/07/lebanon-syria-assyrian-christian-woman-isis-captured-release.html#.

Raqqa is being slaughtered silently, www.raqqa-sl.com/en/.

Reil, James, Q &A: 'Probing Islamic State's sex atrocities with the United Nations', Middle East Eye, May 18, 2015, www.middleeasteye.net/news/qa-probing-islamic-state-s-sex-atrocities-united-nations-1064004421#sthash.jAUSk4yU.dpuf

Richards, Chris, 'Shocking video shows ISIS fighters bartering for young women at "slave girl market"', Daily Record, November 4, 2014, www.dailyrecord.co.uk/news/uk-world-news/shocking-video-shows-isis-fighter-4562374.

Saltman, Erin Marie and Smith, Melanie, '"Till Martyrdom do us part." Gender and the ISIS Phenomenon', Institute for Strategic Dialogue, 2015, www.strategicdialogue.org/Till_Martyrdom_Do_Us Part_Gender_and_the_ISIS_Phenomenon.pdf.

Sanderson, A. B., '"Slavery for Dummies": ISIS Publishes Horrific Guide for Sex Slave Owners', The Counter Jihad Report, December 10, 2014, http://counterjihadreport.com/2014/12/10/slavery-for-dummies-isis-publishes-horrorific-guide-for-sex-slave-owners/.

'Saja al-Dulaimi, Baghdadi's ex-wife and ISIS' prima militant?', Al Arabiya News, February 22, 2015, http://english.alarabiya.net/en/perspective/profiles/2015/02/22/Saja-al-Dulaimi-Baghdadi-s-ex-wife-and-ISIS-s-prima-militant-.html.

'Senior female ISIS agent unmasked and traced to

Seattle', Channel 4, April 28, 2015, www.channel4.com/news/female-isis-women-girl-umm-waqqas-unmasked-seattle.

Variyar, Mugdha, 'Syria: Yazidi Girl Infected with AIDS After Rape by ISIS Fighter; Disease Spreads to Other Members, Say Activists', International Business Times, June 24, 2015, www.ibtimes.co.in/syria-yazidi-girl-infected-aids-after-rape-by-isis-fighter-disease-spreads-other-members-say-636887.

Winter, Charlie (translation and analysis), 'Women of the Islamic State. A manifesto of women by the Al-Khanssaa Brigade', Quilliam Foundation, 2015, www.quilliamfoundation.org/wp/wp-content/uploads/publications/free/women-of-the-islamic-state3.pdf/

Wolf, Mat and Mohammed, Aso, 'Shia-Sunni family from Mosul tells of terror under ISIS', Rudaw, March 25, 2015, http://rudaw.net/english/middleeast/iraq/250320154

Youssef, Nancy A. and Harris, Shane, 'The Women Who Secretly Keep ISIS Running', The Daily Beast, July 5, 2015, www.thedailybeast.com/articles/2015/07/05/the-women-who-secretly-keep-isis-running.html?source=TDB&via=FB_Page.

Zelin, Aaron Y., 'Women of The Islamic State: Beyond the Rumor Mill', Jihadology, March 31, 2015, http://jihadology.net/2015/03/31/guest-post-women-of-the-islamic-state-beyond-the-rumor-mill/.

*All monetary figures mentioned in this book are based on the current exchange rate on August 20, 2016.

The Good Terrorist

By Judit Neurink

Rose's husband is lost in the Caliphate. Her lover, who is also his best friend, goes searching. Will Rose loose them both, or will good win from evil?

Chapter 1

Rose has already scrolled on, as is her habit with pictures of fighters who have earned the honoured status of a martyr by dying a violent death.

Supporters of radical Muslim groups post pictures on social media of bearded men, or of boys too young to sprout more than a couple of hairs on their chin. Taken just before their death, with their right index finger raised in a vow to their God. And sometimes after, of their lifeless bodies. Or of the attack that killed them.

She has gotten used to it, as she has followed these radical groups on Twitter for some time now, ever since one of her students suddenly left for Syria. But today, her subconscious is triggered by something in the picture. As soon as she reloads the image on her mobile screen, she knows why. Shocked, she stares at the familiar face, so different behind the full black beard, with long hair half-hidden under a dark scarf.

Rose puts the phone away, gets up and sits down again. She enlarges the picture. Those eyes, almost black and without any emotion. The mouth set in a determined line. Legs planted securely on the ground, in black pants that leave the man's ankles free. His right arm raised in the religious sign with the stretched index finger, the other arm hanging loosely by the side of the long, Afghani-style shirt. A gun is slung over the shoulder.

Black, black, black.

In the kitchen, she gulps down a glass of water from the tap. Her hands shake, and her heart seems to have sunk into her stomach.

As she leans against the counter, her mind races. She takes deep breaths to steady herself, but they hardly seem to work. She is a practical woman. Her students think she is a rock. How can she let herself be so unhinged by a silly picture on Twitter?

For a moment, she is reminded again of her

student. In reaction to his sudden disappearance, she had made it her task to try and understand the radicalization process of boys like him. Though she had not really succeeded, it made her feel better. She had perhaps missed some clues, but she convinced herself that it was not her fault. There was no way she could have stopped him.

But that was nothing compared to this.

She would recognize this man out of thousands. The posture, the eyes, the look on his face.

Uninvited, her memory offers her a kaleidoscope of images: of Ahmed in shorts at the seaside, with their dog Djin playing next to him; Ahmed playing soccer with his sons, shouting out advice and cheering at the soccer field; Ahmed cooking, with a glass of wine next to him and pop music playing; Ahmed at the dinner table, in discussion with his friends; Ahmed fighting back tears as the vet puts Djin to sleep...

Ahmed, who is as secular as any Moroccan could be, who arrived in Europe at the age of eighteen – and now he would be with these monsters, whom he despised so openly? It is simply not possible. She cannot have been this mistaken, all those years at his side. This isn't Ahmed.

Who is trying so hard to shock her out of her wits? One of her students, perhaps? The sense of humour of some of those teenagers is beyond comprehension.

But why would they? None of them bears her any

grudges. She straightens out and puts the glass away. Full of purpose, she goes to her study. She can't let this scare her. She simply needs to understand it.

Seated at her desk, she searches on her computer for the picture. Now it is big enough to show details that she had not noticed before. The black flag behind him, famous for the radicals of ISIS. The film of yellow dust on his black sports shoes. The black circles under his eyes. The red welt on his cheekbone. The missing button of his shirt. The dirty bandage on the wrist next to his side.

And the caption: 'Abu Mustafa al Hollandi's Martyr's death against the Kurdish unbelievers near Gwer. May Allah accept him.'

The father of Mustafa from the Netherlands... Rose stares at the name, in shock. Ahmed's eldest son is called Mustafa. It would be an appropriate nom de guerre.

She becomes aware of her clenched fists, and relaxes them. Really, this must be a case of mistaken identity. Whatever would bring him to join a bunch of Muslim extremists? How can she believe that is him? Rose has never met anyone as allergic to all things radical and Islam as he is.

The empty eyes of the man in black keep staring back at her from the screen. Who is this? It cannot be him. Unless... Her heart is beating faster when she enlarges the image still further. She can hardly look at it. Because there, next to his eye, is the tiny scar, witness of how as a boy he almost lost an eye when diving near the sharp rocks of the Moroccan northern coast. She touches the screen. Her fingers remember the little dimple in his skin.

Only now, it hits her in full. This is her Ahmed. And he is dead. He has blown himself to bits.

The contents of her stomach rise to her throat. Rose can only just make it to the bathroom in time. With teary eyes, she looks at herself in the mirror.

The man she loved, with whom she fought until there was nothing left to quarrel about, who shaped her life like no one else until they split up almost a year ago – that man has blown himself to bits for a place in heaven, taking others with him into death. The love of her past life is a murderer.

'No,' she says angrily. It simply does not fit: her Ahmed - a suicide killer? 'He would never do that.' Could he have changed that much since they split up? No way. Rose will not allow herself to even consider that thought. She cannot face its consequences.

She rinses her mouth and washes her face under the cold tap. 'So, what happened?' she asks her image in the mirror. In her white face, the bloodshot blue eyes stare back at her. As she automatically runs her hands through her short blond hair to liven it up a bit, she tells herself it is simple enough to manipulate a picture. Add a caption, put it on Twitter and it becomes a reality.

That calms her down a bit, but doesn't stop the

questions from coming. Why would anyone do that, and who then? Did Ahmed somehow make enemies?

Back on her computer, she searches for his last emails. Months ago, he wrote the first one, from the refugee camp in Turkey where he had gone to work as a volunteer. A change she had not been able to fully comprehend-- why would a computer engineer suddenly leave a top job to go and care for Syrian refugees in a foreign camp? Or was it because he too had not been able to deal with their divorce?

Feelings of guilt creep up on her. She should definitely have questioned him about it. How is it possible she didn't? She has four emails in total, sent with a couple of weeks in between. After that, he stopped contacting her. Because she never replied.

And why, why not? Guiltily, Rose stares at the last email, where he asks her again to restore the contact between them. Where he tells her how much he misses her. "Rosie," he writes, "I cannot do it without you."

She is touched by the words. How can it be that she did not react to them at the time? Didn't these words have that effect then too?

I miss you too, Ahmed. I should have told you that. Perhaps then all this would not have happened, and you would have simply returned to Amsterdam. We could have had a new chance together.

But wasn't that the exact reason why she had completely ignored the emails? She had not wanted the umpteenth new chance to be disappointed – because they would get stuck again in their old habits. In their old fights. For it seemed they simply could not live together without those arguments she hated.

She had wanted to start a new relationship with a new man, but had not been able to find someone to fill the gap. Perhaps her feelings for Ahmed had gotten in the way, she now realizes. For she could not live with him, but at the same time not without him either. I cannot do it without you... the same was true for her too.

Her eyes fill with tears. She blew it. He might be dead. And that's her fault. She should have taken him back. That thought makes her so aware of missing him that it hurts.

For a moment, she lets the tears go. Then, remembering the task she has set for herself, she shakes her head and blows her nose. She walks to the kitchen. There, she searches for the tea pot in the cupboard. Strong tea, the way Ahmed always made it, that's what she needs now. It won't bring him back though. Or perhaps a little. If only that were possible.

While she waits for the kettle to boil, she tells herself that she can still make amends. That she must find him. She will send him an email. Or perhaps she has a phone number of that camp in Turkey?

Back to the computer. Disappointed, she notes

there is no recent number in his emails. And her mobile doesn't provide any number other than the one that she must have dialed a million times. Now, a female voice tells her that the number is not in use.

Replying to his last email, her fingers run across the keyboard. "Dear Ahmed, I hope all is well with you. Please phone me as soon as possible." She hesitates, and then adds, "I miss you too. Love, Rose." She clicks the send button.

But something keeps bothering her. What if it is all true? If it isn't just some fake story? If he really is dead?

She rereads the text underneath the picture. The frontline near Gwer. When she Googles it, she finds that this is a town not too far from Iraq's second city Mosul, where ISIS has had its stronghold since June of 2014. It is part of the frontline between ISIS and the Iraqi Kurdish peshmerga fighters. If he had blown himself up there, then he must have killed a number of them in the process.

For her Master's degree, Rose studied the history of radical Islam, and from her research trips to the region she knows the Middle East well enough, as well as from holidays with Ahmed. But she has never been to Iraq. Only from the news does she know that at this moment in time, in the spring of 2015, ISIS is fighting a war on different frontlines with different enemies.

There, Ahmed could have been one of ISIS's

fighters who died as part of its tactical use of suicide killers. They detonate their belts, or drive into the troops with cars filled with explosives.

She reads that the frontline near Gwer is important for its proximity to the Kurdish capital Erbil, only twenty kilometres away. It is where ISIS's thrust forward was blocked last year, after the Americans started their bombing raids to protect their consulate in Erbil and their nearby military base. Thanks to these air raids, the radical group has suffered some painful losses.

Rose turns away from the computer. The whole idea is still too foreign for her. Restlessly, she gets up and paces back and forth in the room. How could he have ever become entangled with these radicals? She goes back to what she knows from the case of her student. There, factors like not feeling at home played a role, feeling frustrated or discriminated against, searching for an ideal, to turn against the world.

This could not be the case with a grown man like Ahmed. Or is she mistaken? He was frustrated after the divorce. And then this sudden break from his old life to become an aid worker in Turkey...

Rose lets out a frustrated sigh. Perhaps she didn't know him as well as she thought. She forces her restless mind to make a list of certainties. She needs to get a hold on this mess somehow. As a computer expert, Ahmed loves his work. He has plenty of friends, and even more social contacts. He's a man who stands in this world with both feet firmly on the ground. He loves his two sons from his first marriage.

Mustafa and Fuad – would he really leave them behind like this? She has so many memories of the four of them, as he had completely integrated them into their life together. Walks, weekends, holidays spent together since they were kids. Rose feels the loss. Those were his happiest moments, and she had been grateful to share them.

All this doesn't fit the story of Ahmed joining ISIS. Most importantly, Ahmed had been resistant to the faith that was forced upon him as a child. His father, who was an imam, had wanted his son to follow in his footsteps. Almost amused, Rose remembers how Ahmed would joke around with quotes from the Quran when he was drinking with friends. He knew the whole book by heart and he hated it. 'What a waste of space on my hard disk,' he would say. 'If only I could erase it.'

When his ex-wife Mina decided to convert to Islam, he was so angry with her. Rose still wonders if Mina did it to spite him, or even to punish him for leaving her for Rose. It had only driven them further apart.

Walking restlessly in her room, she is reminded of Ahmed's anger when ISIS had taken its first Iraqi city, Falluja. 'How can people in Iraq believe that these thieves can save them and even bring them back to power?' he had lamented. He was shocked that ISIS had the help of people who had been loyal to the disposed dictator Saddam Hussein. 'These are Saddam's people in the cloth of the Islam,' he had said in the flowery language of Arab poems. This kind of sentences was one of those small reasons why she loved him. Like the scar near to his eye.

Rose stops in the middle of the room. 'I loved him,' she says out loud. Realizing with sadness that she used the past tense, she drops to the floor and opens the drawer with her picture albums from before she went digital. She pulls one out. Longing for some solace, she opens it and begins leafing through the pictures. Holiday in Spain. Ahmed in the beautiful Arab gardens of Granada. Her finger follows the outline of his handsome face, at least ten years younger. There is hardly a comparison with that horrid black picture from Twitter. Apart from the little scar. She can almost feel it again under her stroking fingertips.

With a deep sigh, she turns the page. Ahmed in Cordoba, admiring the Mezquita, that beautiful Arab mosque turned into a church. Here they had one of their many fights, she remembers uneasily. Ahmed hated the fact that a cathedral was built inside that impressive mosque. Rose had countered him, saying that at least in that way the rest of the place had remained unaltered.

Why fight over that, Rose now wonders. They were both correct, really. An amused little laugh bubbles up, but then the memory of one of their last arguments about ISIS taking over Falluja returns to her. She had shown understanding for the town to welcome ISIS as its saviour. People had yearned for an end to their miserable state. 'You are so naive,' he had told her, yet again. Offended, she had turned away.

Rattled by the memory, Rose puts the photo album back and shuts the drawer. Ahmed had been harsh with her at times. He had wounded her. Pushed her away. Although mostly, their opinions had not been too far apart. They had just been fighting for the fight. That was what their relationship had boiled down to more and more.

Suddenly exhausted, she stretches out on the rug. Following the centuries-old pattern, she can almost see Ahmed haggle with the salesman in some Moroccan market to get the best price. Her house is still full of memories of fifteen years with him. Uncomfortably full, she thinks, getting up.

She had wanted to break the circle of fighting between them. That's mainly why she had left him. He had agreed, and Rose had thought that he had also accepted their separation. That he too was fed up with their fighting.

Yet he had tried multiple times to keep their former life alive, she realizes with a start. By phoning and mailing, he had tried to keep in contact, wanting to see her, inviting her for meals and outings. Why had she not noticed the intent behind it before? And why did she refuse it all, even ignored those emails from Turkey?

Restless, she walks again to the kitchen. The tea in the pot is now too strong, but she boils some water and adds it to lighten the dark brew in her cup. Looking for the sugar, she realizes what she is doing. She hasn't drunk tea in the Arab way for months now.

'Ahmed, oh boy, Ahmed,' she says to the cup, taking it back to her study. 'Make me understand. I feel so lost.'

The words seem to hang in the air. 'Thieves,' he had said about ISIS. But surely, someone who feels that way would never join the group. Can anyone who had so completely left Islam as Ahmed did, really change so much in just a year? 'No way,' Rose says with a sudden certainty. 'Never.'

She can almost hear him say: 'It must be one of the most backward religions in the world, to hide the beauty of women as if it is a sort of forbidden gift from God.' And: 'Islam is like a long-term prison. If you try to step out, you will be punished and become an outlaw.' For Ahmed knew all too well what danger he would face if he showed himself too openly as a former Muslim.

How often had they discussed it, between

themselves and with their friends? Rose knows that she had been attracted to Ahmed's independent mind and his humour. The value of that lost life together now really affects her. For with all its ups and downs, it had been predominantly happy. She has to admit it now: she really does miss him. And yet, she has denied that in the past year – or perhaps more accurately: she has not allowed herself to realize it.

Gloomily, she drinks the last of the sweet brew. So, that life is gone – Ahmed is gone for good? Wishfully, she checks her email. No, he did not reply.

Her eyes scan his last email once more. "Rosie, I cannot do it without you." Suddenly his words energize her. He would want her to solve this odd puzzle. He would have known how to deal with it. 'You should think out of the box, darling,' he would have said with a smile, 'not everything is predictable, you know.'

Well, that he would die in a terror attack, definitely not. Rose could have imagined anything for Ahmed's life and future, but never that.

Never! It just cannot be true! Her resistance has returned. That picture is fake. And did a friend who is a journalist not repeatedly warn her that one source is no source?

She types 'Abu Mustafa al Hollandi' into the search tool on Twitter and finds a tweet by a certain Umm Hunaifa al- Britani that mentions his martyrdom, adding, 'May Allah accept and be pleased with him'. The woman hides her identity behind a flower. Rose knows that for radical Muslims, no one other than the husband and direct family are allowed to see a woman's face, or even her eyes. This derives from the same rule that obliges women to completely cover themselves with a niqaab or even a burqa.

'Striving towards Paradise' is Umm Hunaifa al-Britani's motto underneath the flower. When Rose reads through her tweets, she understands this is a British woman living in the Caliphate. 'Remember the goal is Jannah, where hardship, sorrow, grief don't exist,' she tweeted. Rose translates for herself: The worldly struggle is only temporary, as the goal is Paradise. That's what ISIS is feeding its recruits. One doesn't live to live and be happy, but to die and go to Paradise.

A Paradise where sorrow does not exist. Again, in her head Rose hears Ahmed saying: 'Let's be happy with this one life and make the best of it. Just imagine that Saint Paul would not open the gate to heaven for you?'

She finds herself smiling. Yes, but Ahmed... then there would be no 72 virgins waiting for you when you blew yourself apart!

Come on! This is nonsense. That is simply why she cannot find any proof, except for the one mention of his death. Abu Mustafa al Hollandi himself does not seem to have had a Twitter account. He does not exist. Or has Twitter deleted it, like it does so often with accounts of activists of radical groups?

Frustrated and slightly desperate, Rose ends her search. Here, out-of-the box thinking is quite impossible. She is staring at the picture again, when her mobile rings. Mustafa. She has not spoken to her stepson for weeks. The divorce has also had its effect on their relationship. For years, he spent weekends at their home. Now, they do not even phone one another. She is happy to hear from him now. This cannot be a coincidence.

'Mus. Hi. Did you see the picture?'

She realizes how she took him by surprise when he simply asks, 'What?', omitting even a greeting.

Oh my God, he doesn't know a thing. She cannot do this by phone. Even though he will have just as hard a time believing this thing about his father as she has. 'Sorry dear. Could you come and see me? There's something I need to tell you.'

'Now? Why?'

'I will tell you when you get here. Jump on your bike,' Rose tells him, trying to keep the strong emotions she feels from her voice.

Full of urgency, she again returns to her computer. She must find something. But even on Facebook she finds no trace at all of Abu Mustafa. A frustrated sigh escapes her. Ahmed would have known how to handle this. For him, the World Wide Web has no secrets.

Then it hits her. That's exactly why she cannot find anything! If he really was with ISIS, he would probably try to hide that. And Ahmed has good knowledge of the dark web. Rose knows that ISIS communicates mainly through channels that are hardly visible. So, it can still be true.

'No, no, no!' Her voice shatters the silence of the room. She doesn't want it to be true!

She feels sorry she has let it slip to Mustafa – how do you tell a son that his father might have joined a terror group? How will he take the news?

Now she is concerned for him, knowing that he was a sensitive teenager. But since finalizing his study in computer science, he seems more stable. For lack of a job, he started working as a volunteer in an asylum seeker's centre. When he speaks about what goes on there, Rose often still hears the sensitive boy he was. Then she wants to hug and hold him, like the child that she tried to compensate for what he was missing at his mother's home. When he became a teenager, he would push her away. 'Act normal,' he would say irritably.

He rings the bell – even though he still has the key. Rose waits for him at the top of the stairs and simply pulls him into a hug. Surprised, he lets her, saying, 'Hey Rose, what's up?'

Inside the room, he looks around, expecting something amiss and not finding it. He scrutinizes her face and repeats with more urgency, 'What's up?

What picture?'

Rose knows she must seem dishevelled, and making things worse, tears well up in her eyes.

'Ahmed,' she says simply, sniffling to regain her control.

'Are you okay? What happened to Dad? An accident?'

Rose represses the need to envelop herself into his warmth and hug him again. What to reply? 'I don't know,' she simply says.

He shakes his head in despair, suddenly reminding Rose so much of his dad, with his dark curls and slim posture, that the tears won't let themselves be repressed anymore.

Now Mustafa is really worried. Awkwardly, he rubs over her arm. 'Calm down, Rose. Please, what happened?'

She knows she needs to calm down, so she grabs a tissue and takes a couple of deep breaths. 'Come.' She takes him into her study, where the black picture is burning into the screen.

He stares at it in disbelief. 'Dad?' Rose tells him what the picture implies. About the tweet of the British ISIS woman. He enlarges the picture, just as she had done before, and stares at it. Clearly baffled, he mumbles: 'It is Dad, isn't it?'

Gently, Rose puts a hand on his shoulder. 'Perhaps it is all fake, Mus,' she tries to comfort him as much as herself. 'But I don't seem to be able to find that out.'

'But he is in Turkey! It hasn't been too long since I received an email.'

Relief flows through Rose. Ahmed has continued to write to Mustafa. There you are, it's all nonsense. Her eyes again fill with tears, but this time she manages to hide them.

Together, they go over what they know of Ahmed's past months. Rose now remembers a phone call of about six months ago. Why did she not think of this before? 'It was about Fuad. Ahmed was looking for a good therapist because he was feeling so depressed.'

Now, she knows that the call might not only have been about his youngest son, but was also meant to restore contact with her. She is angry with herself for the way she handled it. Closing herself off. Protecting herself, but against what? It now seems to be all boomeranging back to her.

'I have not spoken to him since. Apart from those emails from Turkey, I have not heard from him.' No wonder, after how she treated him. Even so, Rose checks her email again. 'And he hasn't yet replied to my last email.'

On his phone, Mustafa pulls up the emails his father wrote to him from the refugee camp. They notice that it is the same number as Rose has. Brief emails written by a busy aid worker about shortage of medicines, the rain that changes the camp into a pool of mud, the arrival of new refugees and their traumas.

'What does an IT guy want from a refugee camp,' Rose wonders.

'But I am actually doing the same,' Mustafa says. 'I am an aid worker too now, although I was educated to work in IT. It's not all that strange.'

Rose reads through the emails on his phone. They sound so normal, so uneventful. Very comforting. But then she recognizes parts that are similar to what he wrote to her. Concerned, she pulls up the emails on her computer again. Yes, they were simply cut and pasted. Why? Because it saved him time?

Think out of the box, Rose. She can almost hear Ahmed say it. But she doesn't want to. She doesn't want it to be true.

'How did he like it out there?' she asks her stepson.

'You know, I don't really know. He was busy, I guess.'

'Nowhere in those emails does he talk about himself, have you noticed?' Rose cannot fool herself, however much she wants to. 'He could have copied this straight from some blogs and websites. He did exactly the same in his emails to me.'

She shows them to Mustafa. 'True,' he says thoughtfully. 'But why should I doubt him?'

I don't want to either, Rose thinks. But if this was

about someone else, she would have no doubt at all that the emails were fake.

'So he wanted us to think that he was in Turkey, while in reality he was in Syria or Iraq?' Mustafa doesn't sound too convinced.

'Perhaps, although I really hope not,' Rose hesitates, but then decides that she cannot protect her stepson anymore. This is far too serious. 'Did you ever notice he had become religious?'

Disgusted, Mustafa shakes his head. 'No way. That's not how he is.'

'Think,' Rose presses him. 'Anything you remember.' More slowly this time, Mustafa again shakes his head.

'Then how does he end up with ISIS?'

'So this picture is for real?'

Rose points to the scar, making an effort to hide the shaking of her hands.

To her surprise, Mustafa is still not convinced. 'This could be photoshopped. You can put his head on someone else's body, can't you?'

They examine the picture, searching for proof of manipulation. But the head really fits the neck. The hands appear to be Ahmed's as well, although his wedding ring is missing. He had never taken that off before. Rose then remembers that radical Muslims consider jewellery prohibited for men.

The shoes? Does she remember those? She points them out to her stepson and is aware of the shock it causes. Agitated, he starts to scroll on his phone. 'Where is it!' Then he hands the phone to her. Rose sees Ahmed and his two sons on the beach. They smile at the photographer. The sand beneath their feet is wet, and a wave can be seen moving in that will reach their shoes. Shoes. Ahmed is wearing the same black ones as in the picture on Twitter.

'We went out for a run. You two had recently separated. I wanted to distract him and made Fuad come along.' Mustafa seems to be replaying the images. 'Right after the picture was taken, the sea got to us. My feet were wet inside my shoes. I remember how proud Dad was, that his shoes were watertight.' He points to the black picture. 'Those same shoes.'

Defeated, they look at each other. Everything points to the picture being real. Denial is no longer an option.

'So, if this is correct, then he is dead,' Mustafa says after a long silence. All his normal bravura has left him.

'No.' Rose stubbornly refuses to accept it. 'Even if he really is in Syria, this picture does not prove he is dead.'

Mustafa nods, visibly relieved. Yet, still somehow, they both feel they are only buying time.

'Would your brother perhaps know more?' Rose wonders.

'No idea, he drove me crazy,' Mustafa says

irritably. 'Every time he came with those fibs about how Muslims are being humiliated and how the Syrians are the victims of the West... I was fed up with it and stopped contacting him. I haven't spoken to him for quite some time now.'

Shocked, Rose asks: 'He has become a Muslim? How did that happen?' Guiltily, she realizes that she has not seen her youngest stepson since the divorce. She has even hardly given him any thought since then. And in the meantime, he changed course completely.

Mustafa tiredly shrugs. 'He had been frequenting a mosque near my mother's house.'

'Nobody stopped him?'

'My mother was actually very happy he had come back to the fold of the only right faith,' Mustafa says with another shrug. 'I guess Dad tried to make him change his mind, but he couldn't.'

Rose tries taking in this new knowledge. She remembers Ahmed always worrying about his sons who were living with their mother, as she had become more strictly religious over time. How often he had tried to step in, succeeding with Mustafa when he had come to live with them for part of the week. But for Fuad he had not been able to do much more than keep an eye on him.

And now Fuad had converted to the very faith that Ahmed loathed. Rose is pretty sure his mother was behind it.

'Ahmed must have been devastated,' she says. 'How could your mother do that...'

Mustafa sends her a look of disgust. 'Because she thinks it will save him from hell,' he says.

Rose knows that he is referring to the time Fuad had gotten caught up with a youth gang. It must have been a couple of years ago already. Then, Ahmed had discussed with her how they could get him out. Together they had made a plan they had carefully executed and that had worked; she remembers their shared pride and relief afterwards. They had not involved Fuad's mother, whose total inability to control her son had led to him joining the gang in the first place.

Ahmed had taken Fuad on a month-long trip, without his phone or any contact with the outside world. When after returning, he had then changed his school, the gang members had lost their power over him.

Even so, Fuad had a past as a small-time criminal. Ahmed had told Rose how much Mina resented that stamp society put on her son. Even more than the fact that his father and Rose were the ones who saved him.

Conversion to Islam would erase his sins though. 'Your mother pushed him.' Rose is suddenly completely sure.

Mustafa looks up from his phone, where he has been scrolling through pictures of Ahmed. 'What?' he says distractedly, showing her one of himself and his dad sharing a water pipe. The atmosphere is hazy with smoke, but also amazingly happy and relaxed. Rose realizes her stepson is going down the same memory lane she was on just now.

She pecks his cheek and gets up, leaving him to it. Engrossed in the pictures, he does not even react.

In the kitchen, she busies herself making coffee, the way she knows he likes it. Like father, like son. They both drink their coffee strong and sweet.

Waiting for the espresso machine to do its work, she is pulled back to her thoughts about Fuad and his mother. If Mina pushed him to conversion to clean up his bill, she must have influenced him too. Rose vividly remembers Ahmed complaining how radical she had become, how she talked with admiration of Al-Qaeda. The radical group Ahmed had considered as evil, just as much as ISIS later.

Why is this so interesting, she asks herself, when I am trying to understand what happened to Ahmed?

I am trying to think outside the box, she tells herself. No, you are rather trying to take your mind off it, she gets back.

Frowning, she returns with the coffee to the study where Mustafa is showing her yet another happy picture of his dad.

'Did Fuad want to go to Syria?' she hears herself ask him.

'Why...' Mustafa asks, surprised. Taking it in, he

says slowly, 'I guess so, but what...' He stops, appalled. They look at each other and see the realization sink in. 'My God, Fuad was totally into ISIS. How could I have missed it?'

Suddenly, Rose knows for sure ISIS recruited Fuad. That's not too strange, as the kid was totally confused. It can't have been too difficult to indoctrinate him and take him to Syria. He fits the profile that Rose at the time of her student's disappearance had made of youth that are vulnerable to radicalization. Could it be that Ahmed saw this coming – and that he wanted to talk to her to find a solution?

He had wanted to save his son once again, and contacted her for help. And she had been nonresponsive. Now she really feels guilty.

'But what is the link to your father?'

Mustafa shakes his head. 'It beats me.'

Rose distractedly stirs her coffee. 'There must be a link.'

'No way,' Mustafa states with confidence. 'Dad would never. This horrible picture is simply a fake.'

This was a segment from 'The Good Terrorist', Judit Neurink's novel about life, love and hate in the Caliphate.

For more information and how to buy the book, go to the author's website:
https://juditneurinkauthor.com/the-good-terrorist/

ABOUT THE AUTHOR

Judit Neurink (1957) is a journalist and author from the Netherlands, a specialist on the Middle East who lived and worked in the Kurdistan Region of Iraq from 2008 to 2019, having witnessed both an economic boom, development and crisis, with the entry of the Islamic group ISIS in the region.
She set up a media center in Kurdistan to train journalists and teach politicians and police how to work with the media. After leaving the center, she worked for Dutch and Belgian newspapers, radio and TV, as well as international media.
She has written ten books, all of them connected to the Middle East, amongst them a novel about the Jews of Kurdistan. She now lives with her two Siamese cats in the Greek capital Athens.

ABOUT THE AUTHOR

Judit Neurink (1957) is a journalist and author from the Netherlands, a specialist on the Middle East who lived and worked in the Kurdistan Region of Iraq from 2008 to 2019, having witnessed both an economic boom, development and crisis, with the entry of the Islamic group ISIS in the region.

She set up a media center in Kurdistan to train journalists and teach politicians and police how to work with the media. After leaving the center, she worked for Dutch and Belgian newspapers, radio and TV, as well as international media.

She has written ten books, all of them connected to the Middle East, amongst them a novel about the Jews of Kurdistan. She now lives with her two Siamese cats in the Greek capital Athens.